百年学府文物菁华

苏州大学博物馆馆藏文物精粹

苏州大学博物馆 编

苏州大学出版社
SOOCHOW UNIVERSITY PRESS

图书在版编目(CIP)数据

百年学府文物菁华:苏州大学博物馆馆藏文物精粹:汉英对照 / 苏州大学博物馆编. —苏州:苏州大学出版社,2011.5
ISBN 978-7-81137-694-4

Ⅰ.①百… Ⅱ.①苏… Ⅲ.①文物—苏州市—图录
Ⅳ.①K872.533

中国版本图书馆 CIP 数据核字(2011)第 072255 号

书　　名	**百年学府文物菁华**
	苏州大学博物馆　编
责任编辑	金振华
出版发行	苏州大学出版社
	(苏州市十梓街 1 号　215006)
印　　刷	苏州恒久印务有限公司
开　　本	890 mm×1 240 mm　1/16
印　　张	17.75
字　　数	222 千
版　　次	2011 年 5 月第 1 版
	2011 年 5 月第 1 次印刷
书　　号	ISBN 978-7-81137-694-4
定　　价	280.00 元

苏州大学版图书若有印装错误,本社负责调换
苏州大学出版社营销部　电话:0512-67258835
苏州大学出版社网址　http://www.sudapress.com

《百年学府文物菁华》编委会

主　编：张朋川　黄维娟

编　委：朱　兰　蔡　晨　叶　晨　王　皓

序

柔风如丝，繁花似锦。一年前的春天，苏州大学博物馆隆重开馆。一年后的今天，作品《百年学府文物菁华——苏州大学博物馆馆藏文物精粹》完成并付梓。手捧这本流光溢彩的画册，仿佛在瞬间跨越了人类发展的历史长河，又仿佛悠然地漫步于吴文化浸润的江南大地，锦帛玉纸，金钩铁划，巧石拙木，古韵今风，跃然于纸，神涌于心。

一个人的存在离不开对自身经历的记忆，一个社会、一个民族的存在同样离不开对自身文化的记忆。博物馆作为文化记忆的载体、文物的聚集地，肩负着传承优秀传统文化、提升人们文化素养和社会文化品位的历史使命。美国诗人朗费罗曾说：艺术是永恒的，时间则是瞬息即逝的。面对一件件历史的艺术品，人们在时空穿梭中比较、沉浸、回味、涵咏，追忆和感念曾经的足迹，寻求智慧与启迪，心灵遂得净化，情感是以陶冶，精神渐次升华。

苏州大学博物馆陈列了学校百年发展历程的宝贵藏品、社会各界的友好赠品和学校教师的个人收藏千余件，于 2010 年 5 月 10 日正式建成并开馆。虽为大学小馆，但启馆至今，亦已有百余批团队、3 万余名国内外友人前来参访，赢得好评无数。在今年建校 111 周年华诞前夕，我校从馆藏千余件文物中遴选了 255 件字画、陶瓷器、石器、青铜器、玉器等精品，以文字和图片的形式予以记录和呈现，使历史文物跨越时空界限，让文化精髓泽被万世黎庶。

衷心感谢广大师生员工、校友、社会贤达和海内外友人在我校博物馆建设中作出的辛勤努力及为丰富其文化内涵而奉献的各种藏品，惟愿这本画册的出版能够使苏州大学在保护文物、服务科教、对外交流、繁荣文化方面有更加积极的探索和更富成效的贡献。同时，我还真诚地希望人们在翻阅这本书时，从心灵深处不断激荡起对人类、对生命、对生活、对精神的无限热爱！

苏州大学博物馆馆务委员会主任　王卓君

2011 年 4 月于苏州大学钟楼

Prologue

While May breeze was bringing out lush blossoms in the air of this University's campus yard,the warm spring of last year witnessed the opening of Soochow University Museum. Almost exactly one year later,the Museum has put together this volume,The Pick of the Historic Relics of Soochow University Museum,for publication. Holding this valuable collection in hand,I feel as if I were breaking up the time bonds and stepping back into the flowing river of human history.Between these pages,one rediscovers the greatness of Wu Culture, admires the ancient and modern art in embroidery, silk-making and paper articles,and enjoys the beauty of various metal,wooden and stone pieces that both please the eye and stir the heart.

If an individual person cannot but live with a memory of his experiences,a community cannot but stand with a collective awareness of its culture. As a place where a community's cultural memories are kept, the museum undertakes a historic mission to carry down the excellence of a cultural tradition and upgrade people's cultural taste. Henry Wadsworth Longfellow,an American poet, once wrote: "Art is long, and time is fleeting."Reading this volume, we find ourselves embarking on a journey that takes us back to different erstwhile times and spaces. Here we compare the relics, ponder over their history and marvel at their beauty. While we look at them one by one, one feels we gain in wisdom, inspiration and more importantly,a purified soul, a remolded temperament and a sublimated spirit.

Soochow University Museum was founded on May 10,2010. At the time,it presented over a thousand exhibits,some of which were University relics from the centennial celebrations while others were donated by friends and faculty members. Modest as it may seem,this Museum has by now received more than 30,000 visitors in hundreds of groups,domestic and international. Many a distinguished guest left the Museum with very fond memories and numerous compliments. This year, to celebrate its 111th anniversary,the University has picked out some 255 pieces from its current inventory. Pictures have been made of these works, be they calligraphy,artistic ceramics and porcelain,or stones,bronze and jade, and captions are provided to enable them to speak to all who come to see them.

We genuinely appreciate the great efforts and generous donations that the University faculty,alumni,scholars,artists and friends both at home and abroad have made to the founding of this Museum. It is my sincere hope that the publication of this book will stand as further proof of the positive and effective efforts that we are making in protecting our historic relics,in promoting arts and social sciences,and in helping develop our culture through opening up to the outside world. I also hope that this book will help inspire in you a greater devotion to and a more dedicated love for human mankind, life and,perhaps,spirituality.

Wang Zhuo-jun
Chairman,Managing Committee of
Soochow University Museum
April,2011,at Clock Tower Mansion,
Soochow University

目录

书画

1. 行书七言/联 清 冒襄 3
2. 草书五言/轴 清 归庄 4
3. 行书七言/轴 清 宋曹 5
4. 行书七言/联 清 姚鼐 6
5. 草书五言/轴 清 姚鼐 7
6. 行书五言二十四首/卷 清 张问陶 8–9
7. 楷书论书法/轴 清 阮元 10
8. 临颜鲁公/轴 清 包世臣 11
9. “培德堂”匾额 清 林则徐 12
10. 楷书八言/联 清 林则徐 13
11. 山居图/轴 清 周莲 14
12. 隶书五言/联 清 杨岘 15
13. 隶书四条(一)/屏 清 俞樾 16
14. 隶书四条(二)/屏 清 俞樾 17
15. 行书七言/联 清 张之洞 18
16. 梅花图/轴 清 吴昌硕 19
17. “师米斋”匾额 民国 吴昌硕 20
18. 隶书七言/联 民国 张祖翼 21
19. 无量寿佛图/轴 民国 郑文焯 22
20. 行书七言/轴 民国 陈三立 23
21. 荷塘鸳鸯图/轴 民国 齐白石 24
22. 行书七言/轴 民国 章炳麟 25
23. 行书佛经/轴 民国 梁启超 26
24. 隶书四言/轴 民国 梁启超 27
25. 松竹水仙图/轴 民国 经亨颐 张大千 28
26. 花卉图/轴 民国 陈衡恪 29
27. 花卉图/轴 民国 何香凝(画) 柳亚子(题字) 30
28. 花鸟图/轴 民国 陈树人 31
29. 行书七言/联 民国 柳亚子 32
30. 行书七言/轴 民国 柳亚子 33
31. 忆丽赋并序/轴 民国 陈运彰 34
32. 赤玉盛开图/横幅 现代 王个簃 35
33. 鲁迅先生像/轴 现代 胡亚光(画) 沈尹默(题字) 36
34. 嵩寿图/横幅 现代 谢孝思 吴敹木 张辛稼 37
35. 仕女图/轴 现代 陈小翠 38
36. 草书二幅/册页 现代 苏渊雷 39
37. 斗雪迎春图/横幅 现代 张辛稼 40
38. 鸬鹚图/横幅 现代 唐云 41
39. 行书七言/轴 现代 费孝通 42
40. 汉柏图/轴 现代 徐子鹤 43
41. 太湖春色图/斗方 现代 宋文治 44
42. 庭园小趣图/轴 现代 杜重划 45
43. 松竹梅图/轴 现代 吴敹木 崔护 张辛稼 46
44. 武夷山图/轴 现代 姚奎 47

石器

1. 穿孔石斧、石镰、石钺、石凿 新石器时代 51
2. 石纺轮 新石器时代 52

陶瓷器

1. 陶拍、陶垫、陶纺轮 新石器时代 55
2. 陶罐 新石器时代 56
3. 屋顶形器盖陶罐 新石器时代 57
4. 双大耳红陶罐 新石器时代 58
5. 网格印纹陶罐 西周 59
6. 网格印纹陶罐 春秋 60
7. 黑皮陶罐 战国 61
8. 灰陶鼎 战国 62
9. 原始瓷甬钟 战国 63
10. 茧形灰陶壶 西汉 64
11. 双大耳灰陶罐 西汉 65
12. 釉陶罐(一) 汉代 66
13. 釉陶罐(二) 汉代 67
14. 陶谷仓 汉代 68
15. 陶奁 汉代 69
16. 釉陶壶 汉代 70
17. 绿釉陶勺 汉代 71
18. 陶井 汉代 72
19. “长乐未央”瓦当 汉代 73
20. 云气纹瓦当 汉代 74
21. 陶屋 汉代 75
22. 青釉立鸟瓷盅 西晋 76
23. 斜方格纹四系青瓷盂 西晋 77
24. 双肩耳瓷罐 西晋 78
25. 青釉四系耳瓷罐 东晋 79
26. 青釉瓷钵 东晋 80
27. 四系青瓷罐 东晋 81
28. 青瓷盘 东晋 82
29. 瓦当 南朝 83
30. 四系青瓷壶 隋代 84
31. 四系青瓷罐 隋代 85
32. 青瓷盅 隋代 86
33. 双系青瓷执壶 唐代 87
34. 越窑青瓷盆 唐代 88
35. 花瓣形青瓷水盂 五代 89
36. 邢窑白瓷小碗 五代 90
37. 莲花刻纹瓷诸葛碗 宋代 91
38. 酱褐釉双耳瓷壶 宋代 92
39. 酱褐釉陶壶 宋代 93
40. 孔雀蓝釉梅瓶 宋代 94
41. 影青瓷碗 宋代 95
42. 影青暗花葵口瓷碗 宋代 96
43. 影青瓷魂瓶 南宋 97
44. 湖田窑影青暗花双鱼瓷碗 南宋 98
45. 银扣刻花云龙纹盘 南宋 99
46. 钧窑小瓷碟 金代 100
47. 影青刻花瓷碗 元代 101
48. 钧窑瓷碗 元代 102
49. 龙泉窑高足碗 元代 103
50. 龙泉窑小瓷盘 元代 104
51. 龙泉窑高圈足瓷碗 明代 105
52. 龙泉窑印花人物瓷碗(一) 明代 106
53. 龙泉窑印花人物瓷碗(二) 明代 107
54. 白瓷瓶 明代 108
55. 青花五彩人物盆底插屏 明代 109
56. 德化窑暗花碗 明代 110
57. 青花瓷碗 明代 111
58. 青花花卉纹瓷碗 明代 112
59. 青花人物纹瓷碗 明代 113
60. 青花瓷汤匙 明代 114
61. 青花瓷罐 明代 115
62. 三彩小罐 明代 116
63. 琉璃云龙纹瓦当 明代 117
64. 琉璃龙纹瓦当(一) 明代 118
65. 琉璃龙纹瓦当(二) 明代 119
66. 磁州窑瓷寿星像 明代 120
67. 五彩瓷盘 清代顺治年间 121
68. 豇豆红瓷盘 清代雍正年间 122
69. 青花瓷盘 清代雍正年间 123
70. 豇豆红瓷盘 清代乾隆年间 124
71. 茶叶末瓷瓶 清代 125
72. 祭红瓷瓶 清代 126

73. 石榴红瓷盂 清代 127
74. 斗彩瓷碟 清代 128
75. 青釉瓷花瓶 清代 129
76. 青花瓷罐 清代 130
77. 瓷塑 清代 131
78. 德化窑三足炉 清代 132
79. 白瓷三足炉 清代 133
80. 建窑瓷马蹄杯 清代 134
81. 瓷花瓶 清代同治年间 135
82. 蓝双兽耳琮式瓷瓶 清代光绪年间 136
83. 蟠龙纹瓷坛 清代光绪年间 137

俑

1. 陶鸡 汉代 141
2. 陶猪 汉代 142
3. 陶马头 汉代 143
4. 彩绘武士陶俑(一) 北魏 144
5. 彩绘武士陶俑(二) 北魏 145
6. 陶马(一) 北魏 146
7. 陶马(二) 北魏 147
8. 陶骆驼 北魏 148
9. 陶镇墓兽 北魏 149
10. 彩绘戴风帽陶俑 北魏 150
11. 武士陶俑 北朝 151
12. 釉陶女俑 隋代 152
13. 陶俑 隋代 153
14. 彩绘文官陶俑 唐代 154
15. 陶文俑头像 唐代 155
16. 陶侏儒俑 唐代 156
17. 陶男俑(一) 唐代 157
18. 陶男俑(二) 唐代 158
19. 陶男俑(三) 唐代 159
20. 陶男俑(四) 唐代 160
21. 陶女俑 唐代 161
22. 彩绘男侍陶俑(一) 唐代 162
23. 彩绘男侍陶俑(二) 唐代 163
24. 彩绘男侍陶俑(三) 唐代 164
25. 彩绘男侍陶俑(四) 唐代 165
26. 彩绘男侍陶俑(五) 唐代 166
27. 彩绘女侍陶俑(一) 唐代 167
28. 彩绘女侍陶俑(二) 唐代 168
29. 彩绘女侍陶俑(三) 唐代 169
30. 彩绘女侍陶俑(四) 唐代 170
31. 彩绘女侍陶俑(五) 唐代 171
32. 侍女陶俑 唐代 172
33. 陶鸡 唐代 173
34. 人物瓷俑(一) 宋代 174
35. 人物瓷俑(二) 宋代 175
36. 人物瓷俑(三) 宋代 176
37. 人物瓷俑(四) 宋代 177

铜器

1. 铜戣 周代 181
2. 蟠螭纹夔纹铜鼎 战国 182
3. 错银铜车辖 战国 183
4. 铜铃 战国 184
5. 铜戈(一) 战国 185
6. 铜戈(二) 战国 186
7. 铜戈(三) 战国 187
8. 铜鼎 西汉 188
9. 四蟠龙纹铜镜 西汉 189
10. 铜舟 汉代 190
11. 铜洗 汉代 191
12. 铜壶 汉代 192
13. 铜剑 汉代 193
14. 铜弩机 汉代 194
15. 铜大吉铃 汉代 195
16. 规矩纹铜镜 汉代 196
17. 西王母人物铜镜 东汉 197
18. 对鸟纹铜镜 六朝 198
19. 五福双喜湖州造铜镜 宋代 199
20. 荷花纹铜镜 宋代 200
21. 湖州石氏铜镜 宋代 201
22. “无像”铜镜 宋代 202

23. "广武县酒务记"铜印 宋代 203
24. "映湖"铜印 宋代 204
25. 海兽葡萄纹镜 明代 205
26. 铜宣德炉(一) 清代 206
27. 铜宣德炉(二) 清代 207
28. 铜宣德炉(三) 清代 208
29. 大刀(一) 清代 209
30. 大刀(二) 清代 210

玉器

1. 玉佩饰 商代 213
2. 玉瑱 商代 214
3. 玉谷纹璧 战国 215
4. 玉压脐 汉代 216
5. 玉饰 汉代 217
6. "∏"形玉饰 汉代 218
7. 玉马 南朝 219
8. 玉雕鹭鸶荷花片 明代 220
9. 玉龙纹透雕牌 明代 221
10. 玉斋戒片 清代 222
11. 玉鲤鱼跳龙门纹璧 清代 223
12. 玉环柄杯 清代 224
13. 玉寿星 清代 225
14. 玉如意 清代 226

钱币

1. 安邑布币 战国 229
2. 五字刀(即墨之法化) 战国 230
3. "垣"字钱币 战国 231
4. "大泉五十"钱范 新莽 232
5. 大观通宝 宋代 233
6. 洪武通宝 明代 234
7. 太平天国铜钱 清代 235

杂项

1. 骨珠 商代 239
2. 骨簪 商代 240
3. 绳纹陶井圈 汉代 241
4. 铜佛像(一) 北朝 242
5. 铜佛像(二) 北朝 243
6. 铜佛像(三) 北朝 244
7. 鎏金铜佛像 北朝 245
8. 隋开皇二年石佛造像 隋代 246
9. 鎏金铜佛造像 北宋 247
10. 骨蟠龙方牌 明代 248
11. 陶瓮 明代 249
12. 筒瓦砚 清代乾隆年间 250
13. 木雕观音像 清代 251
14. 竹雕花鸟压纸 清代 252
15. 螺钿盘 清代 253
16. 木尺 清代 254
17. 字典木刻板(一) 清代 255
18. 字典木刻板(二) 清代 256
19. 吴大澂所用石砚 清代 257

参考文献 259

Contents

Painting and Calligraphy

1. Couplet of Seven Character Poem in Running Script *Qing Dynasty, Mao Xiang* 3
2. Scroll of Five Character Poem in Cursive Script *Qing Dynasty, Gui Zhuang* 4
3. Scroll of Seven Character Poem in Running Script *Qing Dynasty, Song Cao* 5
4. Couplet of Seven Character in Running Script *Qing Dynasty, Yao Nai* 6
5. Scroll of Five Character Poem in Cursive Script *Qing Dynasty, Yao Nai* 7
6. Scroll of 24 Poems in Five Character Script in Running Style Calligraphy *Qing Dynasty, Zhang Wentao* 8-9
7. Scroll in Regular Script about Calligraphy *Qing Dynasty, Ruan Yuan* 10
8. Calligraphic Scroll Imitating the Style of Yan Lugong *Qing Dynasty, Bao Shichen* 11
9. Inscription:" Pei De Tang" *Qing Dynasty, Lin Zexu* 12
10. Compliments Couplet of Eight Character Poem in Regular Script *Qing Dynasty, Lin Zexu* 13
11. Mountain Landscape Scroll *Qing Dynasty, Zhou Lian* 14
12. Couplet of Five Character Poem in Clerical Script *Qing Dynasty, Yang Xian* 15
13. Four Calligraphic Scrolls in Clerical Script(Ⅰ) *Qing Dynasty, Yu Yue* 16
14. Four Calligraphic Scrolls in Clerical Script(Ⅱ) *Qing Dynasty, Yu Yue* 17
15. Couplet of Seven Character Poem in Running Script *Qing Dynasty, Zhang Zhidong* 18
16. Plum Bloom Painting *Qing Dynasty, Wu Changshuo* 19
17. Inscription: "Shi Mi Zhai" *Republic of China, Wu Changshuo* 20
18. Couplet of Seven Character Poem in Clerical Script *Republic of China, Zhang Zuyi* 21
19. Buddha of Infinite Life *Republic of China, Zheng Wenzhuo* 22
20. Scroll of Seven Character Poem in Running Script *Republic of China, Chen Sanli* 23
21. Painting of Mandarin Ducks on a Lotus Flower Pond *Republic of China, Qi Baishi* 24
22. Scroll of Seven Character Poem in Running Style *Republic of China, Zhang Binglin* 25
23. Sutra in Running Script *Republic of China, Liang Qichao* 26
24. Scroll of Four Character Poem in Clerical Script *Republic of China, Liang Qichao* 27
25. Painting of Pine Trees, Bamboos and Daffodils *Republic of China, Jing Hengyi, Zhang Daqian* 28

26. Vertical Painting Scroll of Flowers *Republic of China, Chen Hengque* 29
27. Vertical Painting Scroll of Flowers
Republic of China, He Xiangning, with an Inscription by Liu Yazi 30
28. Painting of Birds and Flowers *Republic of China, Chen Shuren* 31
29. Couplet of Seven Character Poem in Running Script *Republic of China, Liu Yazi* 32
30. Scroll of Seven Character Poem in Running Script *Republic of China, Liu Yazi* 33
31. Verse of Yi Li and the Preface *Republic of China, Chen Yunzhang* 34
32. Horizontal Scroll of Cherry-apple in Full Bloom *People's Republic of China, Wang Geyi* 35
33. Vertical Scroll Portrait of Mr. Lu Xun
People's Republic of China, Hu Yaguang, with an Inscription by Shen Yinmo 36
34. Horizontal Scroll Painting of Longevity
People's Republic of China, Xie Xiaosi, Wu Yangmu, Zhang Xinjia 37
35. Painting of a Maid *People's Republic of China, Chen Xiaocui* 38
36. Two Pieces of Calligraphy in Cursive Script *People's Republic of China, Su Yuanlei* 39
37. Spring Snow Painting *People's Republic of China, Zhang Xinjia* 40
38. Horizontal Scroll Painting of Cormorants *People's Republic of China, Tang Yun* 41
39. Scroll of Seven Character Poem in Running Script
People's Republic of China, Fei Xiaotong 42
40. Vertical Panting of Chinese Cypress *People's Republic of China, Xu Zihe* 43
41. Painting of Spring on the Taihu Lake *People's Republic of China,Song Wenzhi* 44
42. Fun in the Courtyard *People's Republic of China, Du Chonghua* 45
43. Painting of Pine Bamboo Plum
People's Republic of China, Wu Yangmu, Cui Hu, Zhang Xinjia 46
44. Vertical Painting of Mount Wuyi *People's Republic of China, Yao Kui* 47

Stoneware

1. Perforated Axes, Stone Sickle, Perforated Zax, Stone Chisel *The Neolithic Age* 51
2. Stone Spinning Wheel *The Neolithic Age* 52

Pottery and Porcelain

1. Pottery Bat, Pottery Pad, Pottery Spinning Wheel *The Neolithic Age* 55
2. Pottery Pot *The Neolithic Age* 56
3. Pottery Jar with Roof-shaped Cover *The Neolithic Age* 57
4. Red Pottery Pot with Double Big Handles *The Neolithic Age* 58
5. Mesh-Checked Pottery Pot *The Western Zhou Dynasty* 59
6. Mesh-Checked Pottery Pot *The Spring and Autumn Period* 60
7. Black Pottery Crock *The Warring States* 61

8. Grey Pottery Tripod *The Warring States* 62
9. Protoporcelain Bells *The Warring States* 63
10. Cocoon-shaped Grey Pottery Kettle *The Western Han Dynasty* 64
11. Grey Pottery Vessel with Double Big Handles *The Western Han Dynasty* 65
12. Glazed Pottery Pot(Ⅰ) *Han Dynasty* 66
13. Glazed Pottery Pot(Ⅱ) *Han Dynasty* 67
14. Pottery Barn *Han Dynasty* 68
15. Pottery Casket *Han Dynasty* 69
16. Glazed Pottery Pot *Han Dynasty* 70
17. Green-glazed Pottery Spoon *Han Dynasty* 71
18. Pottery Well *Han Dynasty* 72
19. Eaves Tiles with Epigraph "Endless Joy" *Han Dynasty* 73
20. Eaves Tiles with a Design of Clouds *Han Dynasty* 74
21. Pottery House *Han Dynasty* 75
22. Green-glazed Porcelain Bowl with a Design of a Standing Bird *The Western Jin Dynasty* 76
23. Slanting-mesh-pattern Celadon Jar with Four Handles *The Western Jin Dynasty* 77
24. Porcelain Pot with Double Handles *The Western Jin Dynasty* 78
25. Green-glazed Porcelain Jar with Four Handles *The Eastern Jin Dynasty* 79
26. Green-glazed Porcelain Alms Bowl *The Eastern Jin Dynasty* 80
27. Celadon Pot with Four Handles *The Eastern Jin Dynasty* 81
28. Celadon Plate *The Eastern Jin Dynasty* 82
29. Eaves Tiles *Southern Dynasty* 83
30. Celadon Kettle with Four Handles *Sui Dynasty* 84
31. Celadon Pot with Four Handles *Sui Dynasty* 85
32. Celadon Wine-cup *Sui Dynasty* 86
33. Celadon Ewer with Double Handles *Tang Dynasty* 87
34. Yue Kiln Celadon Pot *Tang Dynasty* 88
35. Petal-patterned Celadon Water-jar *The Five Dynasties* 89
36. Xing Kiln White Porcelain Bowl *The Five Dynasties* 90
37. Zhu-Ge Porcelain Bowl with a Design of Lotus *Song Dynasty* 91
38. Black-brown-glazed Pottery Kettle with Double Handles *Song Dynasty* 92
39. Black-brown-glazed Porcelain Kettle *Song Dynasty* 93
40. Peacock-blue-glazed Vase *Song Dynasty* 94
41. Shadowy Blue Porcelain Bowl *Song Dynasty* 95
42. Shadowy Blue Sunflower-shaped Porcelain Bowl *Song Dynasty* 96
43. Shadowy Blue Porcelain Vase *The Southern Song Dynasty* 97

44. Double-fish-patterned Shadowy Blue Porcelain Bowl from Hu Tian Kiln *The Southern Song Dynasty* 98

45. Porcelain Plate with a Design of Dragon *The Southern Song Dynasty* 99

46. Jun Kiln Small Porcelain Dish *Jin Dynasty* 100

47. Celadon Porcelain Bowl with a Design of Flower *Yuan Dynasty* 101

48. Jun Kiln Porcelain Bowl *Yuan Dynasty* 102

49. Long Quan Kiln Porcelain Bowl with High Bottom *Yuan Dynasty* 103

50. Long Quan Kiln Small Porcelain Dish *Yuan Dynasty* 104

51. Long Quan Kiln Porcelain Bowl with High Bottom *Ming Dynasty* 105

52. Long Quan Kiln Porcelain Bowl with a Figure Design *Ming Dynasty* 106

53. Long Quan Kiln Porcelain Bowl with a Figure Design *Ming Dynasty* 107

54. White-porcelain Vase *Ming Dynasty* 108

55. Five-color-glazed Figure-stamped Celadon Bottle *Ming Dynasty* 109

56. De Hua Kiln Porcelain Bowl *Ming Dynasty* 110

57. Stamped Blue-and-white Porcelain Bowl *Ming Dynasty* 111

58. Stamped Celadon Bowl with a Pattern of Flowers *Ming Dynasty* 112

59. Stamped Celadon Bowl with a Figure Pattern *Ming Dynasty* 113

60. Stamped Blue-and-white Porcelain Spoon *Ming Dynasty* 114

61. Stamped Blue-and-white Porcelain Pot *Ming Dynasty* 115

62. Three-color Pot *Ming Dynasty* 116

63. Color-glazed Eaves Tile with a Design of Dragon *Ming Dynasty* 117

64. Color-glazed Eaves Tile with a Design of Dragon(Ⅰ) *Ming Dynasty* 118

65. Color-glazed Eaves Tile with a Design of Dragon(Ⅱ) *Ming Dynasty* 119

66. Porcelain God of Longevity from Ci Zhou Kiln *Ming Dynasty* 120

67. Five-color-glazed Porcelain Plate *Shunzhi's Reign of Qing Dynasty* 121

68. Cowpea Red Porcelain Dish *Yongzheng's Reign of Qing Dynasty* 122

69. Stamped Celadon Bowl *Yongzheng's Reign of Qing Dynasty* 123

70. Cowpea-red Porcelain Dish *Qianlong's Reign of Qing Dynasty* 124

71. Tea-dust Glazed Porcelain Bottle *Qing Dynasty* 125

72. Red Porcelain Vase *Qing Dynasty* 126

73. Garnet Porcelain Jar *Qing Dynasty* 127

74. Polychrome Porcelain Dish *Qing Dynasty* 128

75. Blue-glazed Porcelain Vase *Qing Dynasty* 129

76. Blue-and-white Porcelain Jar *Qing Dynasty* 130

77. Porcelain Figurine *Qing Dynasty* 131

78. Three-legged Censer from De Hua Kiln *Qing Dynasty* 132

79. Three-legged White Porcelain Censer *Qing Dynasty* 133

80. Horseshoe Porcelain Cup from Jian Kiln *Qing Dynasty* 134
81. Porcelain Vase *Tongzhi's Reign of Qing Dynasty* 135
82. Porcelain Vase with Double Beast-handles *Guangxu's Reign of Qing Dynasty* 136
83. Porcelain Jug with a Design of Dragon *Guangxu's Reign of Qing Dynasty* 137

Figurine

1. Pottery Chicken *Han Dynasty* 141
2. Pottery Swine *Han Dynasty* 142
3. Pottery Horse Head *Han Dynasty* 143
4. Polychrome Warrior Pottery Figurine(Ⅰ) *The Northern Wei Dynasty* 144
5. Polychrome Warrior Pottery Figurine(Ⅱ) *The Northern Wei Dynasty* 145
6. Pottery Horse(Ⅰ) *The Northern Wei Dynasty* 146
7. Pottery Horse(Ⅱ) *The Northern Wei Dynasty* 147
8. Pottery Camel *The Northern Wei Dynasty* 148
9. Pottery Tomb Beast *The Northern Wei Dynasty* 149
10. Polychrome Capped Pottery Figurine *The Northern Wei Dynasty* 150
11. Warrior Pottery Figurine *Northern Dynasty* 151
12. Color-glazed Maid Pottery Figurine *Sui Dynasty* 152
13. Pottery Figurine *Sui Dynasty* 153
14. Polychrome Pottery Figurine of Civil Official *Tang Dynasty* 154
15. Pottery Figurine *Tang Dynasty* 155
16. Pottery Midget *Tang Dynasty* 156
17. Pottery Man(Ⅰ) *Tang Dynasty* 157
18. Pottery Man(Ⅱ) *Tang Dynasty* 158
19. Pottery Man(Ⅲ) *Tang Dynasty* 159
20. Pottery Man(Ⅳ) *Tang Dynasty* 160
21. Pottery Woman *Tang Dynasty* 161
22. Polychrome Male Servant Pottery Figurine(Ⅰ) *Tang Dynasty* 162
23. Polychrome Male Servant Pottery Figurine(Ⅱ) *Tang Dynasty* 163
24. Polychrome Male Servant Pottery Figurine(Ⅲ) *Tang Dynasty* 164
25. Polychrome Male Servant Pottery Figurine(Ⅳ) *Tang Dynasty* 165
26. Polychrome Male Servant Pottery Figurine(Ⅴ) *Tang Dynasty* 166
27. Polychrome Maid Pottery Figurine(Ⅰ) *Tang Dynasty* 167
28. Polychrome Maid Pottery Figurine(Ⅱ) *Tang Dynasty* 168
29. Polychrome Maid Pottery Figurine(Ⅲ) *Tang Dynasty* 169
30. Polychrome Maid Pottery Figurine(Ⅳ) *Tang Dynasty* 170
31. Polychrome Maid Pottery Figurine(Ⅴ) *Tang Dynasty* 171

32. Pottery Handmaiden *Tang Dynasty* 172
33. Pottery Chicken *Tang Dynasty* 173
34. Porcelain Figurine(Ⅰ) *Song Dynasty* 174
35. Porcelain Figurine(Ⅱ) *Song Dynasty* 175
36. Porcelain Figurine(Ⅲ) *Song Dynasty* 176
37. Porcelain Figurine(Ⅳ) *Song Dynasty* 177

Bronzeware

1. Bronze Lance *Zhou Dynasty* 181
2. Bronze Tripod with a Design of Curling Dragons *The Warring States* 182
3. Silver-bronze Alloy Pin *The Warring States* 183
4. Bronze Bell *The Warring States* 184
5. Bronze Dagger-Axe(Ⅰ) *The Warring States* 185
6. Bronze Dagger-Axe(Ⅱ) *The Warring States* 186
7. Bronze Dagger-Axe(Ⅲ) *The Warring States* 187
8. Bronze Tripod *The Western Han Dynasty* 188
9. Bronze Mirror with a Design of Four Dragons *The Western Han Dynasty* 189
10. Bronze Container *Han Dynasty* 190
11. Bronze Washing Pot *Han Dynasty* 191
12. Bronze Kettle *Han Dynasty* 192
13. Bronze Sword *Han Dynasty* 193
14. Bronze Cross-bow *Han Dynasty* 194
15. Big Bronze Bell *Han Dynasty* 195
16. Bronze Mirror with Regular Designs *Han Dynasty* 196
17. Bronze Mirror with Figure Patterns *The Eastern Han Dynasty* 197
18. Bronze Mirror with a Design of Double Birds *The Six Dynasties* 198
19. Bronze Mirror of Double Happiness and Five Blessings Symbols Made in Hu Zhou *Song Dynasty* 199
20. Bronze Mirror with a Design of Lotus *Song Dynasty* 200
21. Bronze Mirror Made by Shi Family from Hu Zhou *Song Dynasty* 201
22. Bronze Mirror *Song Dynasty* 202
23. Bronze Seal of "Alcohol Bureau of Guangwu County" *Song Dynasty* 203
24. Bronze Seal of "Ying Hu" *Song Dynasty* 204
25. Mirror with a Design of Sea Beast and Grapes *Ming Dynasty* 205
26. Bronze Censer from Emperor Xuande's Reign(Ⅰ) *Qing Dynasty* 206
27. Bronze Censer from Emperor Xuande's Reign(Ⅱ) *Qing Dynasty* 207
28. Bronze Censer from Emperor Xuande's Reign(Ⅲ) *Qing Dynasty* 208

29. Broadsword(Ⅰ) *Qing Dynasty* 209
30. Broadsword(Ⅱ) *Qing Dynasty* 210

Jadeware

1. Jade Pendant *Shang Dynasty* 213
2. Jade Ornaments of Crown *Shang Dynasty* 214
3. Grain-patterned Jade Ornament *The Warring States* 215
4. Jade Ornament *Han Dynasty* 216
5. Jade Ornament *Han Dynasty* 217
6. Jade Ornament *Han Dynasty* 218
7. Jade Horse *Southern Dynasty* 219
8. Jade Egret and Lotus *Ming Dynasty* 220
9. Jade Sculpture of Dragon *Ming Dynasty* 221
10. Jade Plate *Qing Dynasty* 222
11. Carp-through-Dragon-Gate Jade Ornament *Qing Dynasty* 223
12. Jade Cup with Annular Handle *Qing Dynasty* 224
13. Jade Figurine of God of Longevity *Qing Dynasty* 225
14. Jade Symbol of Luck *Qing Dynasty* 226

Coin

1. Cloth Currency of An Yi *The Warring States* 229
2. Bronze Knife-shaped Money *The Warring States* 230
3. "Yuan" Character Coin *The Warring States* 231
4. Coin Mould of "Da Quan Fifty" *Wangmang's New Dynasty* 232
5. Coin of Emperor Daguan's Reign *Song Dynasty* 233
6. Coin of Emperor Hongwu's Reign *Ming Dynasty* 234
7. Bronze Coin of The Taiping Heavenly Kingdom *Qing Dynasty* 235

Sundries

1. Bone Bead *Shang Dynasty* 239
2. Bone Hairpin *Shang Dynasty* 240
3. Ceramic Rope-worn Design Well-Crib *Han Dynasty* 241
4. Bronze Statue of Buddha(Ⅰ) *Northern Dynasty* 242
5. Bronze Statue of Buddha(Ⅱ) *Northern Dynasty* 243
6. Bronze Statue of Buddha(Ⅲ) *Northern Dynasty* 244
7. Gilded Bronze Statue of Buddha *Northern Dynasty* 245
8. Buddha Stone Statue from the Second Year of Kai Huang Period *Sui Dynasty* 246

9. Gilded Bronze Statue of Buddha *The Northern Song Dynasty* 247
10. Plate with a Design of Curling Dragon *Ming Dynasty* 248
11. Pottery Niche *Ming Dynasty* 249
12. Inkstone *Qianlong's Reign of Qing Dynasty* 250
13. Wood Statue of Goddess of Mercy *Qing Dynasty* 251
14. Bamboo Paperweight with a Design of Flowers and Birds *Qing Dynasty* 252
15. Plate Inlaid with Mother-of-pearl *Qing Dynasty* 253
16. Wood Ruler *Qing Dynasty* 254
17. Wood Mould of Dictionary(Ⅰ) *Qing Dynasty* 255
18. Wood Mould of Dictionary(Ⅱ) *Qing Dynasty* 256
19. Wu Dacheng's Inkstone *Qing Dynasty* 257

References 259

书画

Painting and Calligraphy

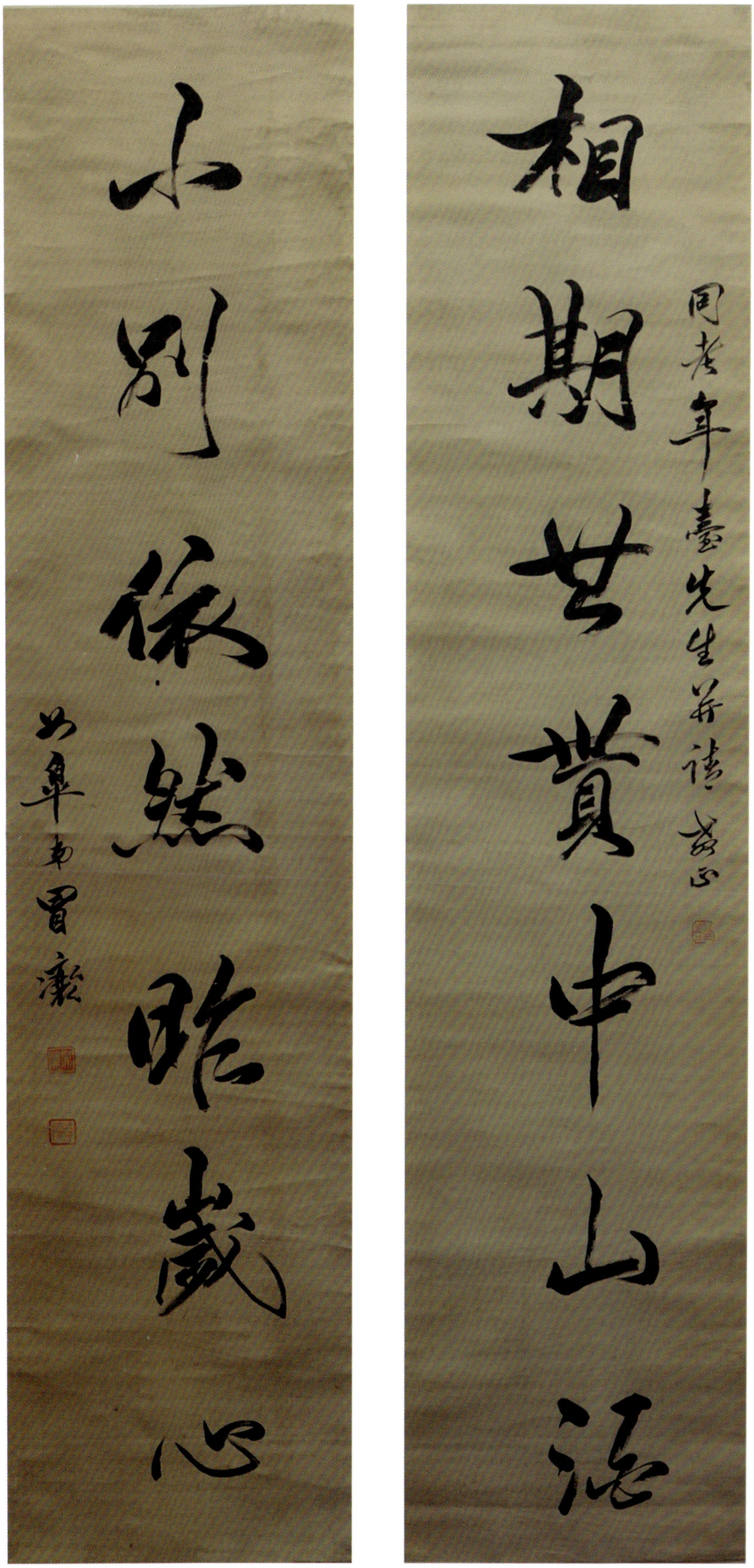

1. 行书七言 联
Couplet of Seven Character
Poem in Running Script

清　　冒　襄
Qing Dynasty, Mao Xiang

纵 139 厘米　横 30 厘米

释文：相期共贯中山酒
　　　小别依然昨岁心

冒襄（1611—1693），字辟疆，号巢民、朴庵，私谥潜孝先生。江苏如皋人。其行、草无不擅长，书法放荡而不失法度，整体如行云流水，一气呵成。

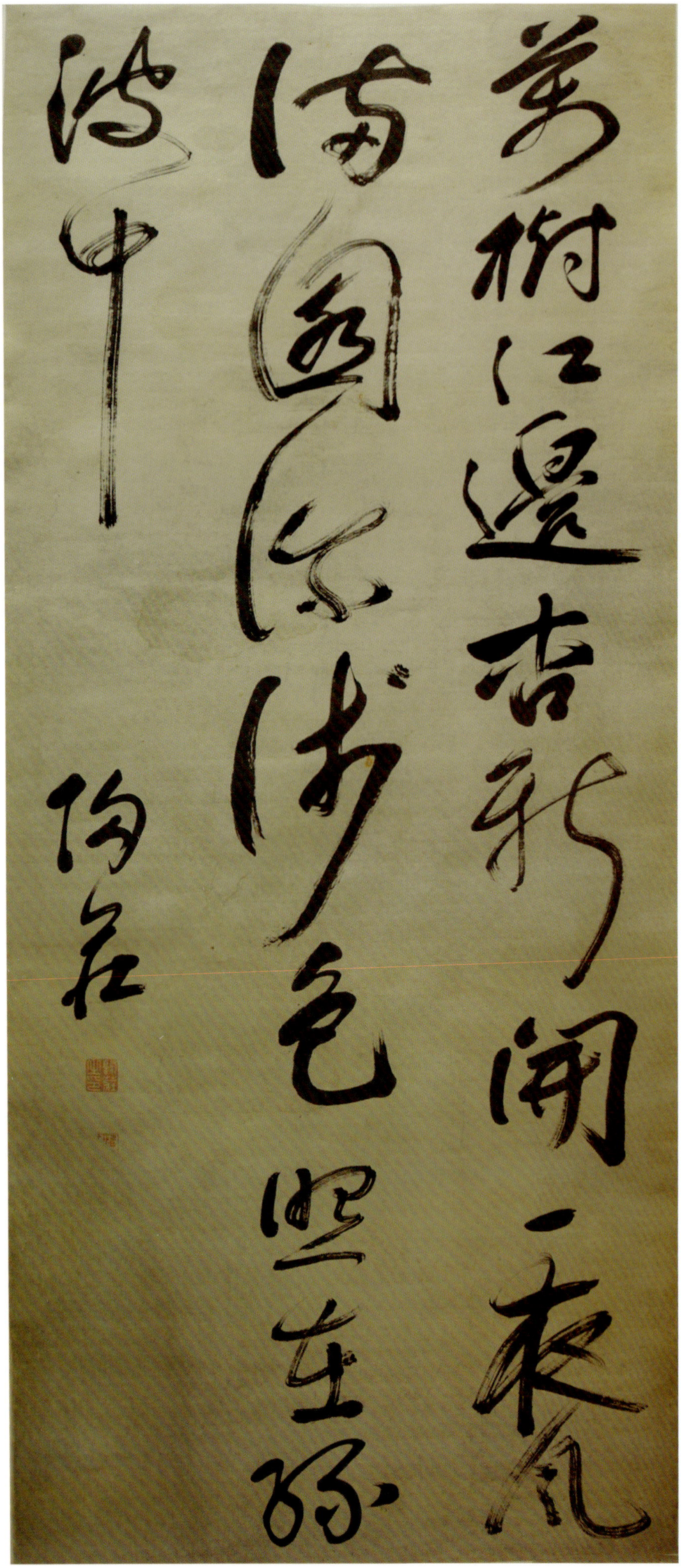

2. 草书五言 轴
Scroll of Five Character Poem in Cursive Script

清　归　庄
Qing Dynasty, Gui Zhuang

纵 166 厘米　横 66 厘米

释文：万树江边杏 新开一夜风
　　　满园深浅色 照在绿波中

归庄(1613—1673)，字玄恭，号恒轩，江苏昆山人。文辞、书、画，奄有众长，善行草书，杨宾称其草书虚和圆熟，吴伟业亦盛称之。亦善大书。

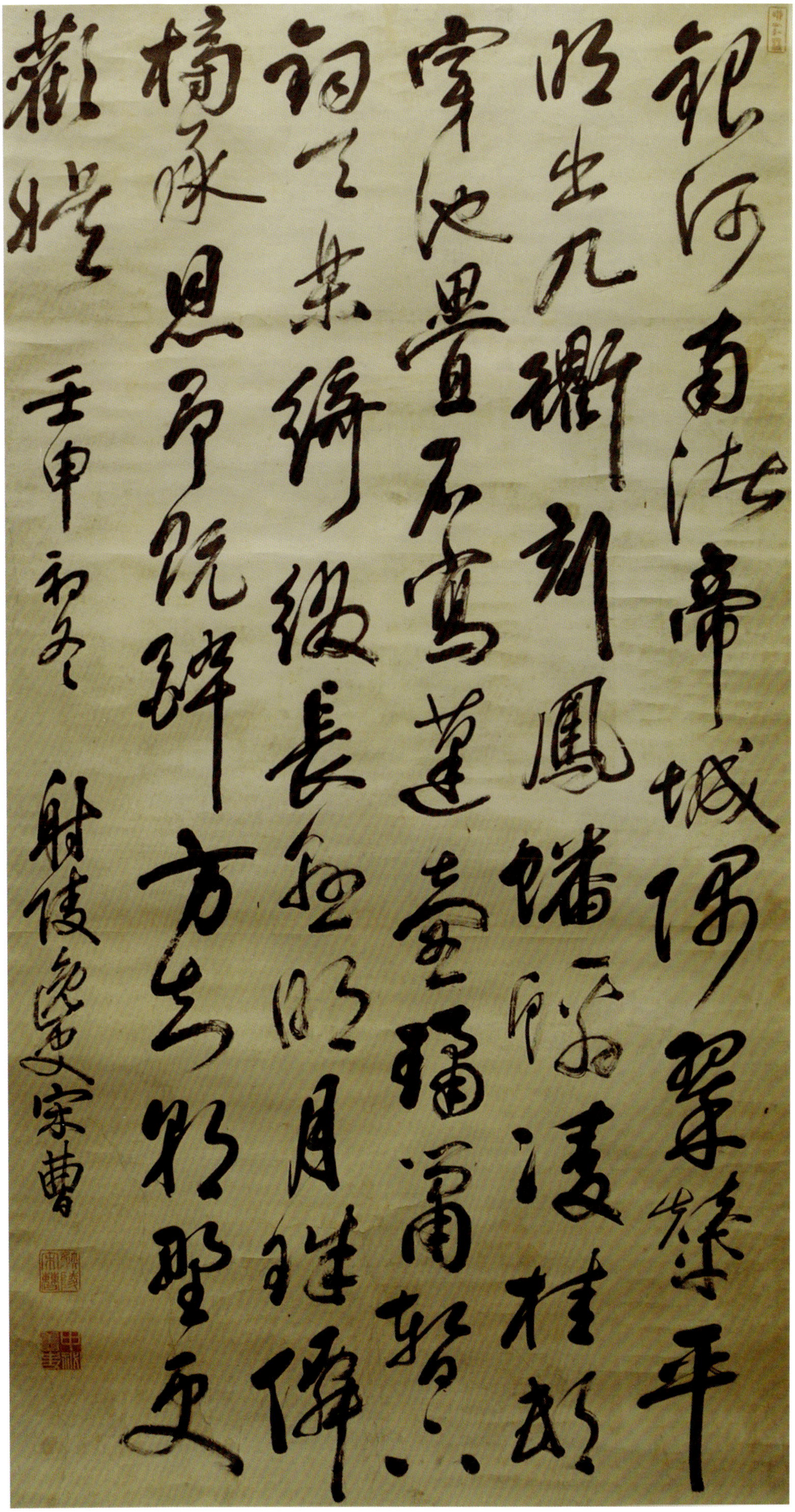

3. 行书七言 轴
Scroll of Seven Character Poem in Running Script

清　宋曹
Qing Dynasty, Song Cao

纵 166 厘米　横 85 厘米

释文：银河南渚帝城隅
翠辇平明出九衢
刻凤蟠螭凌桂邸
穿池叠石写蓬壶
琼箫暂下钧天乐
绮缀长悬明月珠
仙榜承恩争既醉
方知朝野更欢娱

宋曹（1620—1701），字彬臣，号射陵，江苏盐城人。明崇祯时，官至中书舍人。著有《书法约言》，工书能文，尤精书法。其书法具有粗犷、豪迈之气。

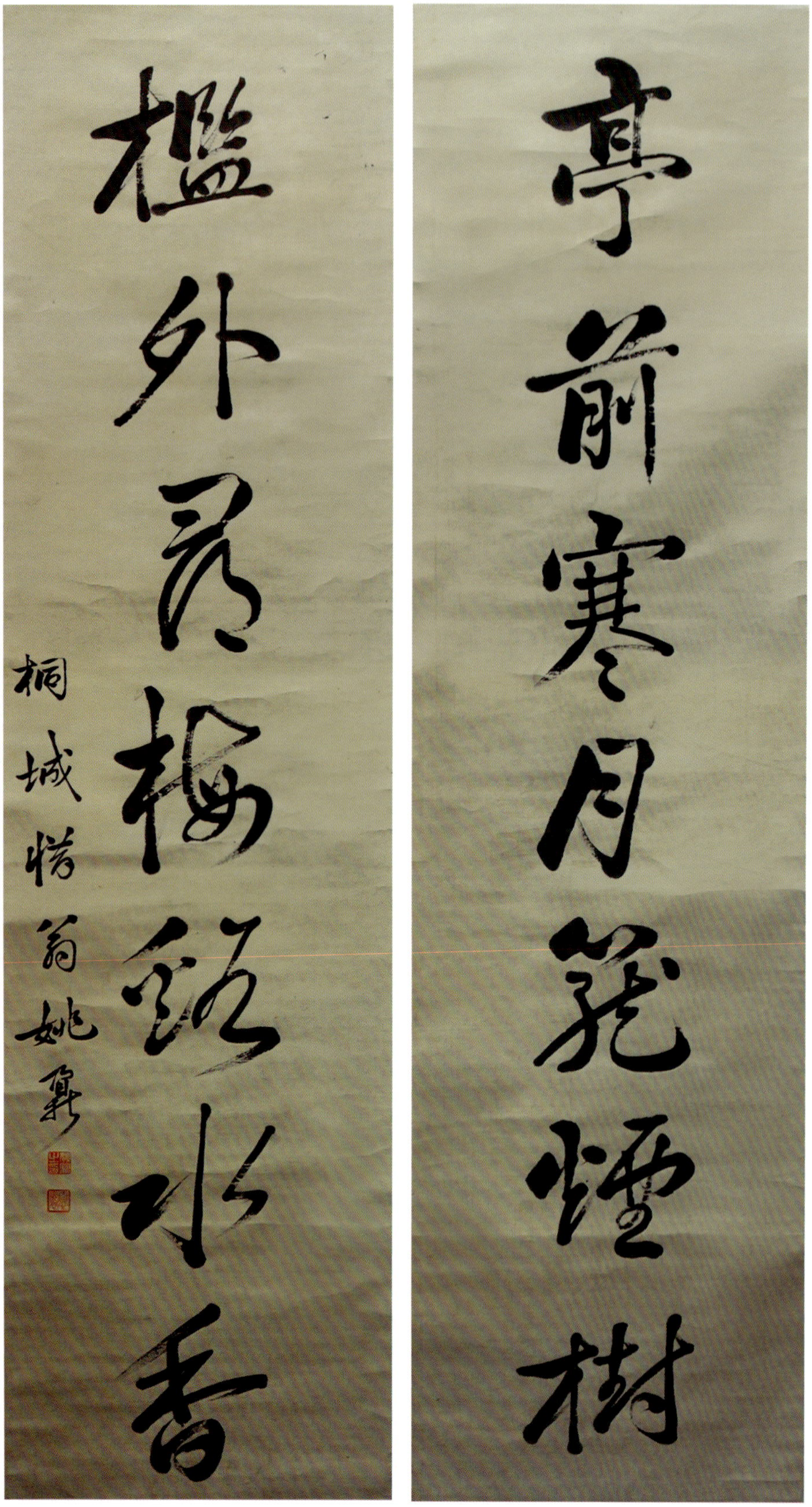

4. 行书七言 联
Couplet of Seven Character in Running Script

清　　姚　鼐

Qing Dynasty,Yao Nai

纵 150 厘米　横 39 厘米

释文：亭前寒月笼烟树
　　　槛外落梅溪水香

姚鼐(1731—1815)，字姬传，号惜抱，安徽桐城人。专精王献之，为方寸行草，宕逸而不空怯。其半寸以内真书，洁净而能恣肆，多所自得。

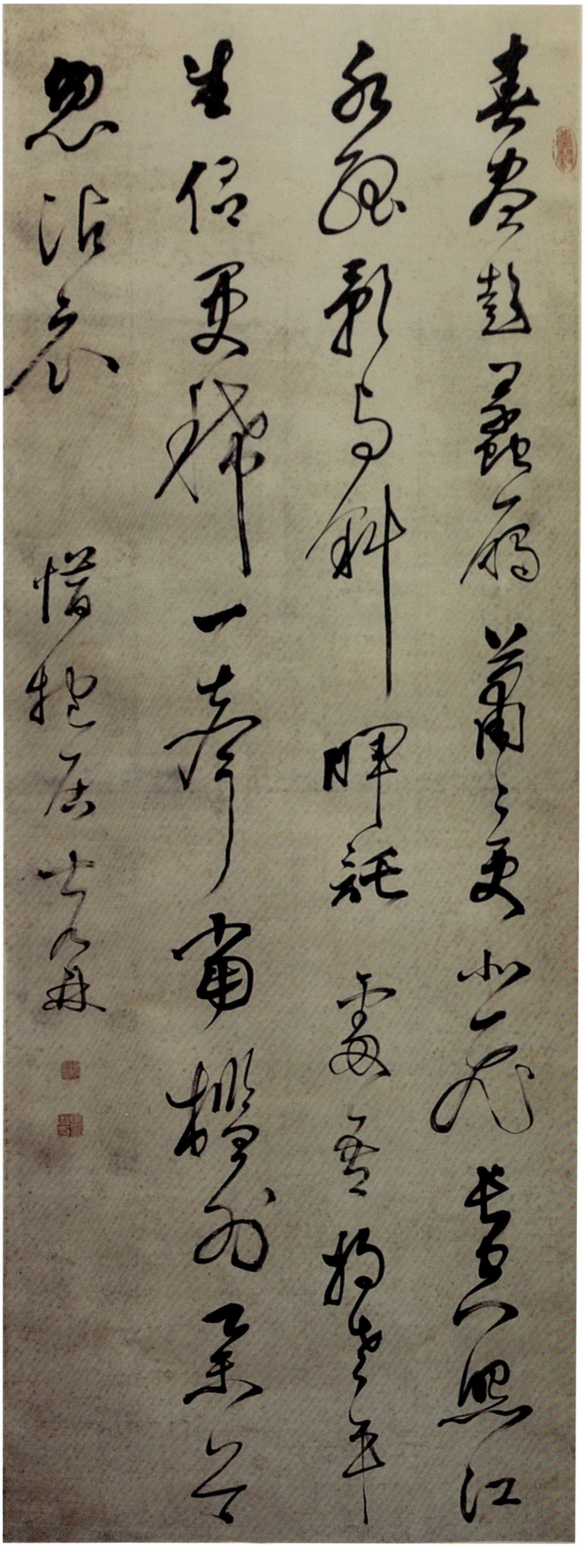

5. 草书五言 轴
Scroll of Five Character Poem in Cursive Script

清　姚鼐
Qing Dynasty, Yao Nai

纵 128.7 厘米　横 47 厘米

释文：春尽彭蠡雁 萧萧更北飞
长空照江水 孤影与斜晖
托处吾将老 平生侣更稀
一声啸槛外 举首忽沾衣

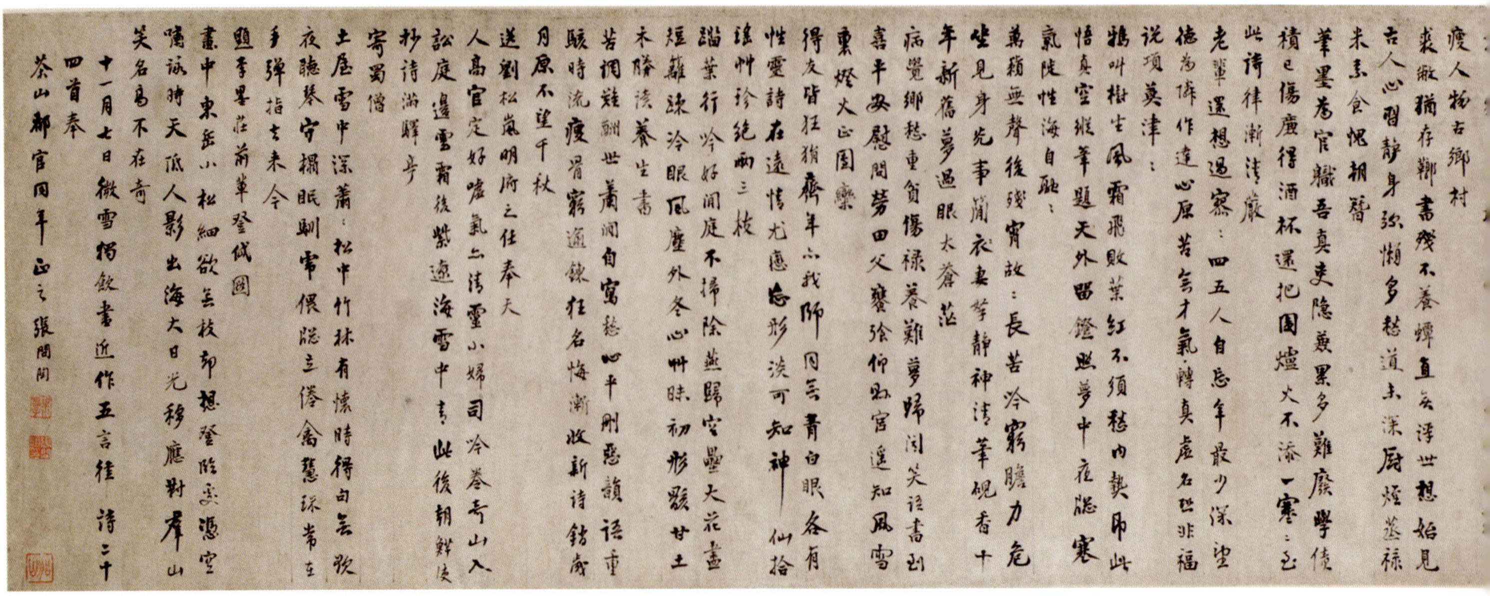

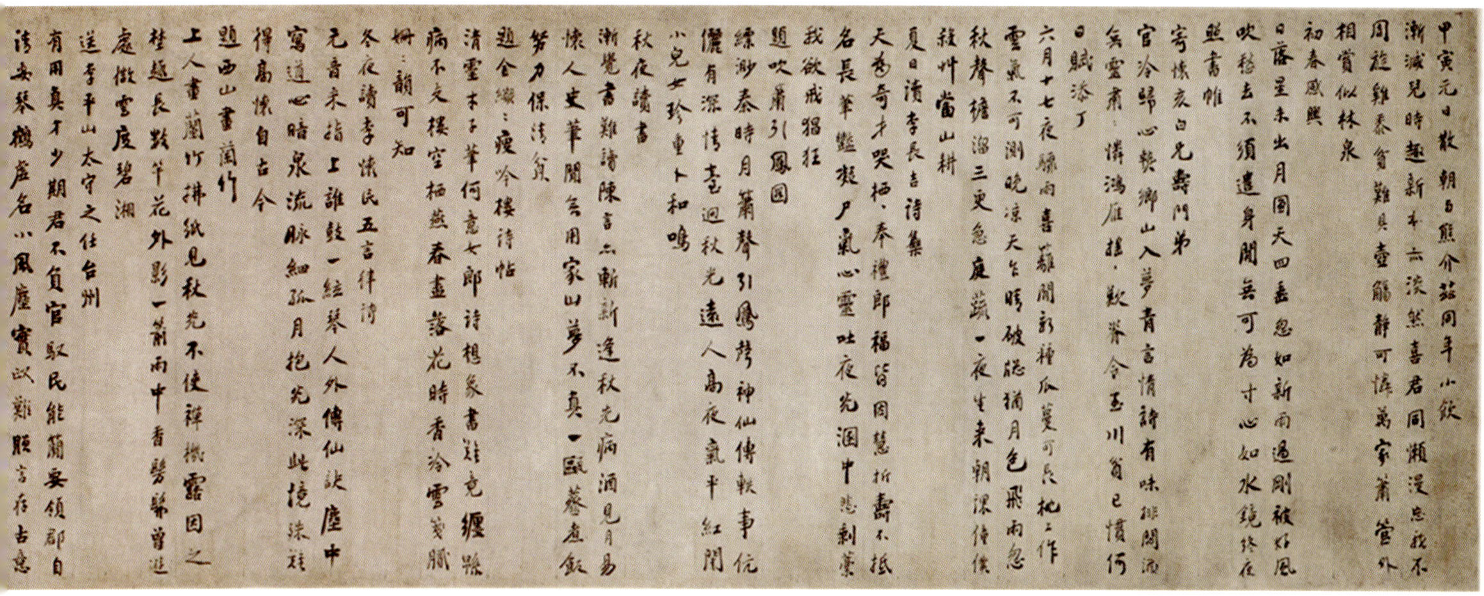

6. 行书五言二十四首 卷
Scroll of 24 Poems in Five Character Script in Running Style Calligraphy

清　张问陶
Qing Dynasty, Zhang Wentao

纵 37.5 厘米　横 200 厘米

张问陶(1764—1814),字仲冶,号船山,又号蜀山老猿、药庵退守。四川遂宁人,侨居江苏苏州。书师米芾,曾为乾隆写养心殿屏。笔意沉郁空灵,骨力内蕴,饶有意趣。

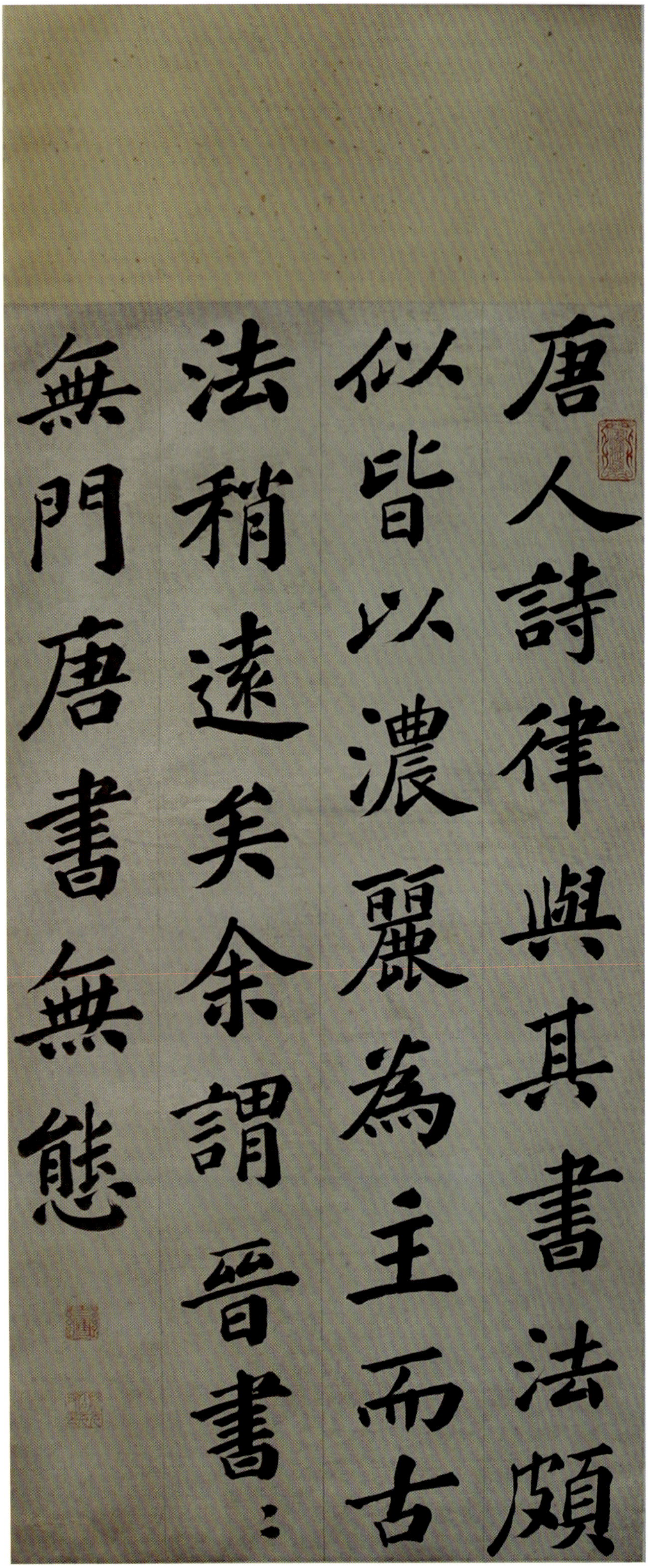

7. 楷书论书法 轴

Scroll in Regular Script about Calligraphy

清　　阮　元

Qing Dynasty, Ruan Yuan

纵 111.8 厘米　横 56.5 厘米

释文：唐人诗律 与其书法颇似
　　　皆以浓丽为主 而古法稍远矣
　　　余谓晋书无门 唐书无态

阮元(1764—1849),字伯元,号芸台,又号雷塘庵主,晚号怡性老人,江苏仪征人。工诗文,精鉴金石、书、画,善篆、隶、行、楷。所作书,郁盘飞动,间仿天发神谶碑。

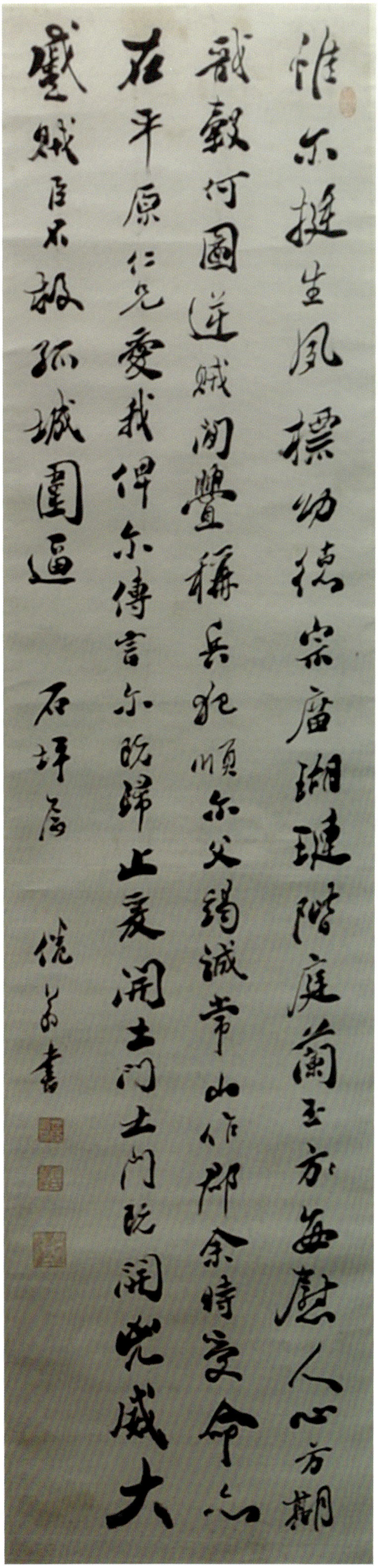

8. 临颜鲁公 轴
Calligraphic Scroll
Imitating the Style of Yan Lugong

清　　包世臣
Qing Dynasty,Bao Shichen

纵 173 厘米　横 40 厘米

释文：惟尔挺生 夙标幼德 宗庙瑚琏 阶庭兰玉 方…… 每慰人心
方期戬谷 何图逆贼闲衅 称兵犯顺 尔父竭诚 常山作郡
余时受命 亦在平原 仁兄爱我 俾尔传言 尔既归止
爰开土门 土门既开 凶威大蹙 贼臣不救 孤城围逼

包世臣(1775—1855),字诚伯,号慎伯,晚号倦翁,安徽泾县人。邓石如弟子,得邓派真传,中年书从颜、欧,后肆力北魏,晚习二王,遂成绝业。书法、篆刻为当代所推服。

9. “培德堂”匾额
Inscription:“Pei De Tang”

清　　林则徐
Qing Dynasty,Lin Zexu

纵 63 厘米　横 187 厘米

林则徐(1785—1850),字少穆,一字元抚,晚号竢村老人,福建侯官(今福州)人。善行草,以《集王圣教序》为基本路数,属传统派系,通篇秀劲,乃其可贵之处。

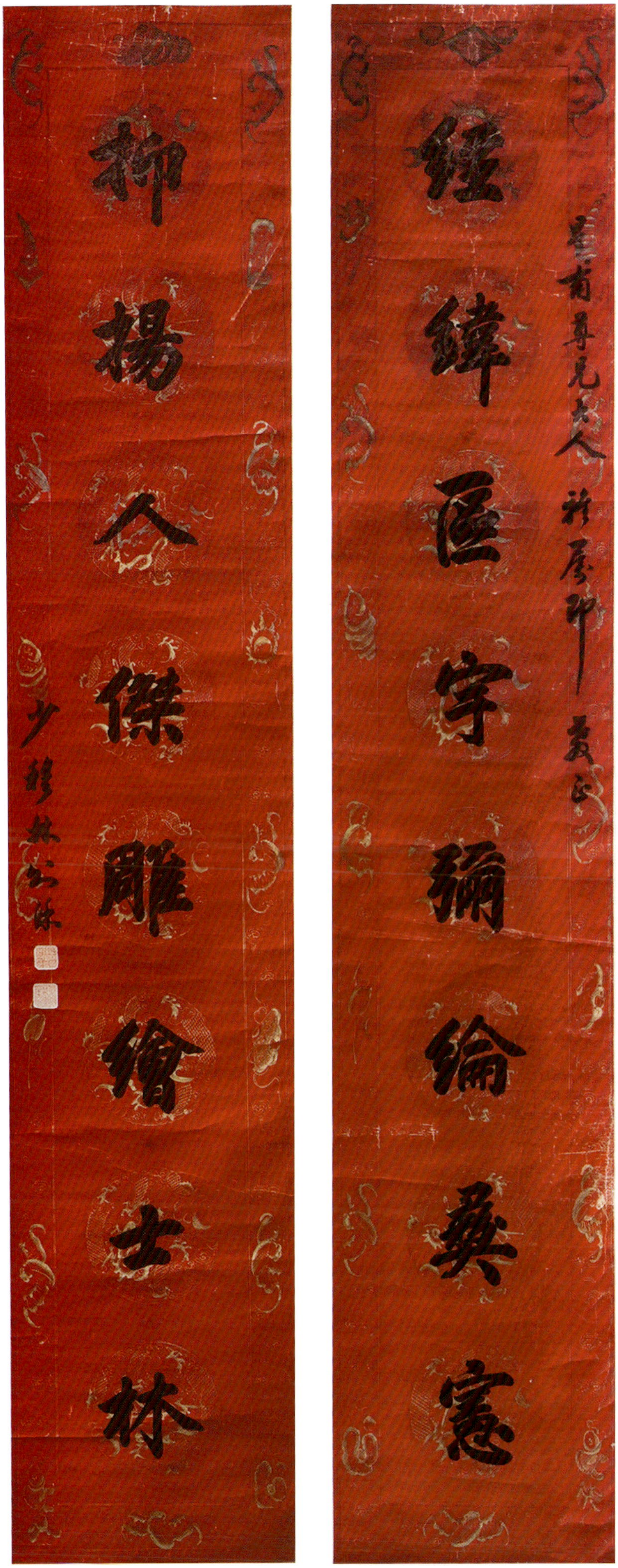

10. 楷书八言 联
Compliments Couplet of Eight Character Poem in Regular Script

清　　林则徐
Qing Dynasty,Lin Zexu

纵 231 厘米　横 43 厘米

释文：经纬区宇弥纶彝宪
　　　抑扬人杰雕绘士林

这对楷书八言联，尺幅巨大，书法严谨，为林则徐书写对联的代表作。

11. 山居图 轴
Mountain Landscape Scroll

清　　周　莲

Qing Dynasty, Zhou Lian

纵 87.5 厘米　横 21.5 厘米

周莲(1790—？),字子爱,号叔明,华亭(今上海市松江)人。工诗文,通六法,兼师文、董两家。其画梅尤纵横如意。书兼四体,铁笔秀洁,婉折多姿。

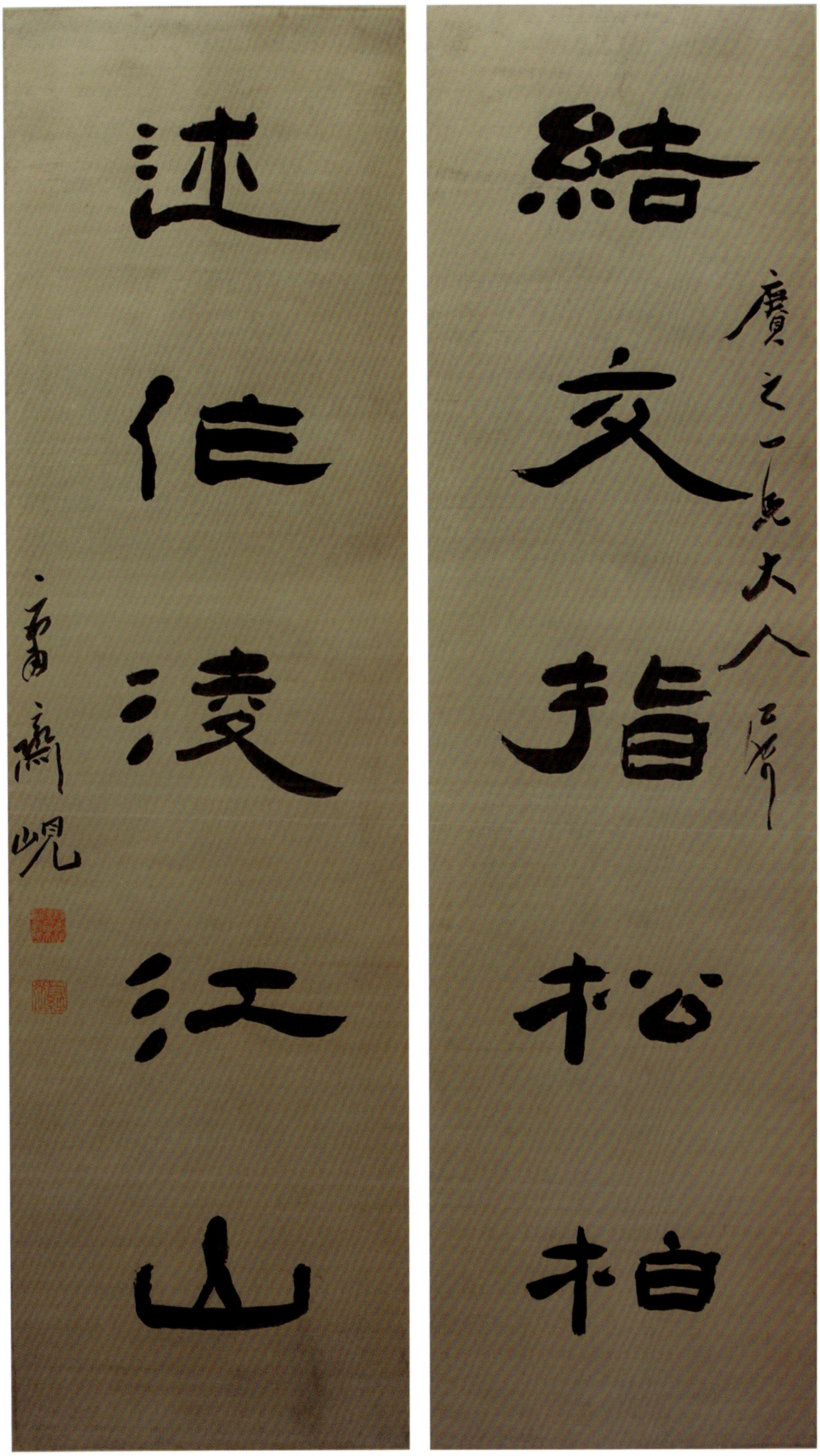

12. 隶书五言 联
Couplet of Five Character
Poem in Clerical Script

清　　杨　岘
Qing Dynasty, Yang Xian

纵 141.5 厘米　横 37.8 厘米

释文：结交指松柏
　　　述作凌江山

杨岘(1819—1896)，字见山，号季仇，晚号藐翁，归安(今浙江湖州)人。咸丰五年(1855)举人，官常州知府。其隶书瘦劲矫健，疏中求密，既强调外形的风采，又力求内涵的充实，在书法界素有“杨隶”之称。

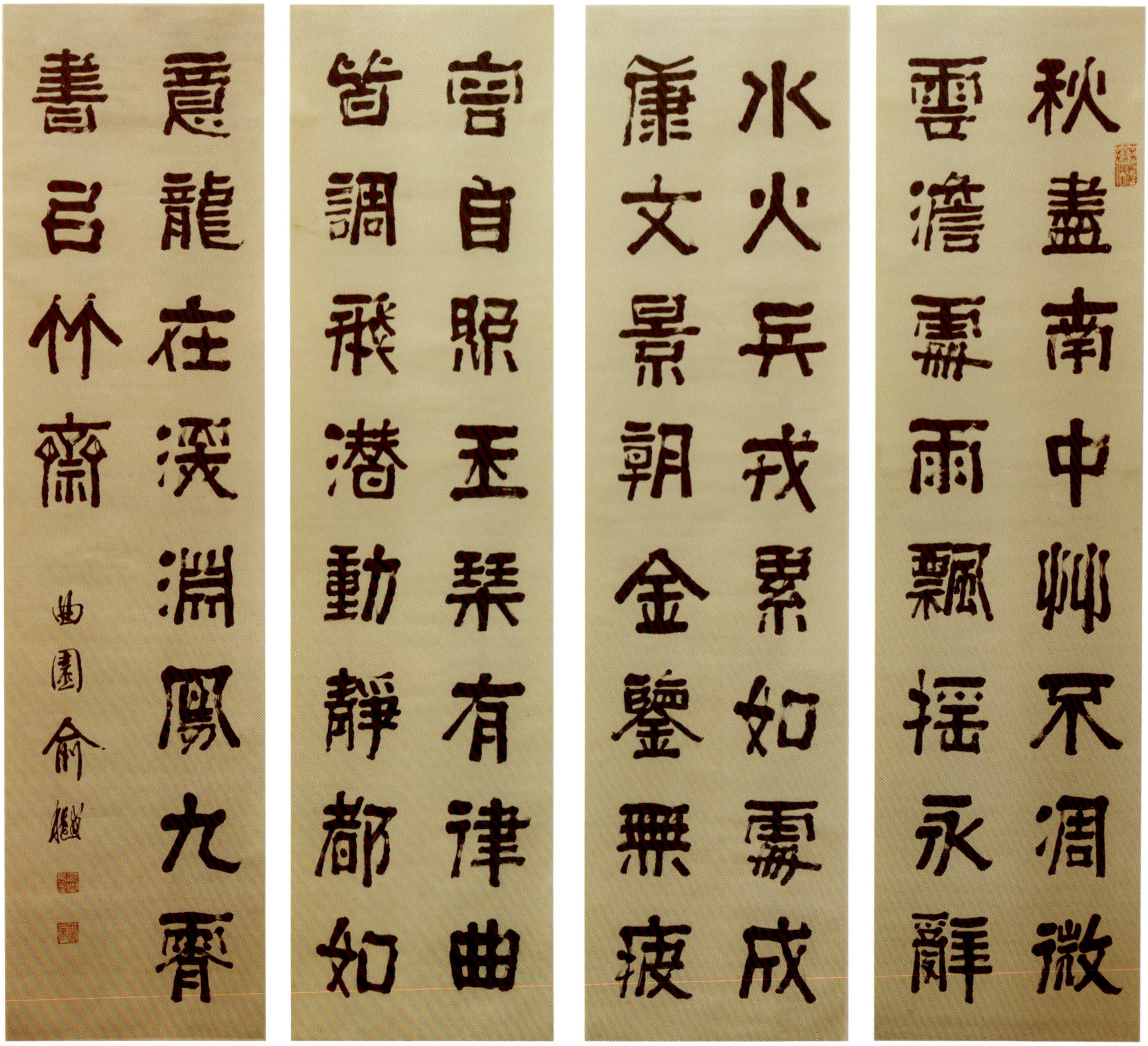

13. 隶书四条(一)屏

Four Calligraphic Scrolls in Clerical Script(Ⅰ)

清　　俞　樾

Qing Dynasty, Yu Yue

纵 134.6 厘米　横 33 厘米

释文：秋尽南中草不凋　微云澹处雨飘摇
永辞水火兵戎累　如处成康文景朝
金鉴无疲曾自照　玉琴有律曲皆调
飞潜动静都如意　龙在深渊凤九霄
书以竹斋

俞樾(1821—1906),字荫甫,号曲园居士,浙江德清人。工书法,有江声之风,以篆、隶法作真书,别具一格。寻常书札,率以隶体书之,尤工大字。

14. 隶书四条(二) 屏

Four Calligraphic Scrolls in Clerical Script(Ⅱ)

清　　俞　樾

Qing Dynasty,Yu Yue

纵 145 厘米　横 38 厘米

释文：建安之初 五言腾踊 文帝陈思 纵辔以骋节
王徐应刘 望路而争驱 并怜风月 狎池苑
述恩荣 叙酣宴 慷慨以任气 磊落以使才
造怀指事 不求纤密之巧

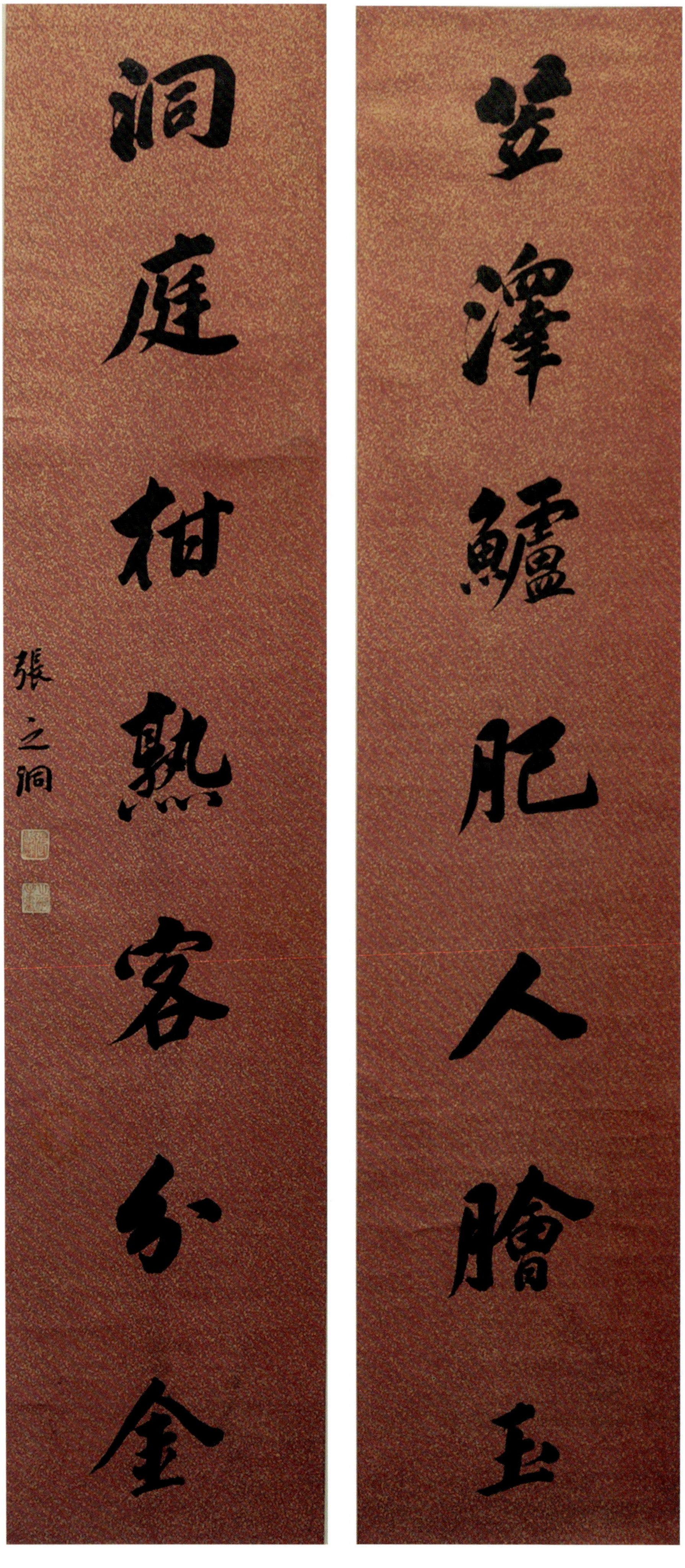

15. 行书七言 联
Couplet of Seven Character Poem in Running Script

清　　张之洞
Qing Dynasty,Zhang Zhidong

纵 132 厘米　横 25 厘米

释文：笠泽鲈肥人脍玉
　　　洞庭柑熟客分金

张之洞(1833—1909),字香涛,号孝达,又字香岩、号壶公,直隶南皮(今属河北)人。同治二年进士,官至体仁阁大学士,卒谥文襄。著广雅堂诗集。工书,笔意开展。

16. 梅花图 轴
Plum Bloom Painting

清末民初　　吴昌硕
Late Qing Dynasty and Early Republic of China, Wu Changshuo

纵 100 厘米　横 41 厘米

吴昌硕(1844—1927),名俊、俊卿,字昌硕、仓石,多别号,常见者有仓硕、老苍等。浙江安吉人。其画笔墨坚挺,气魄厚重,色彩浓郁,结构突兀,一笔一画无不精神饱满,有金石气。

17. “师米斋”匾额

Inscription:“Shi Mi Zhai”

清末民初　　吴昌硕

Late Qing Dynasty and Early Republic of China, Wu Changshuo

纵 44 厘米　横 182 厘米

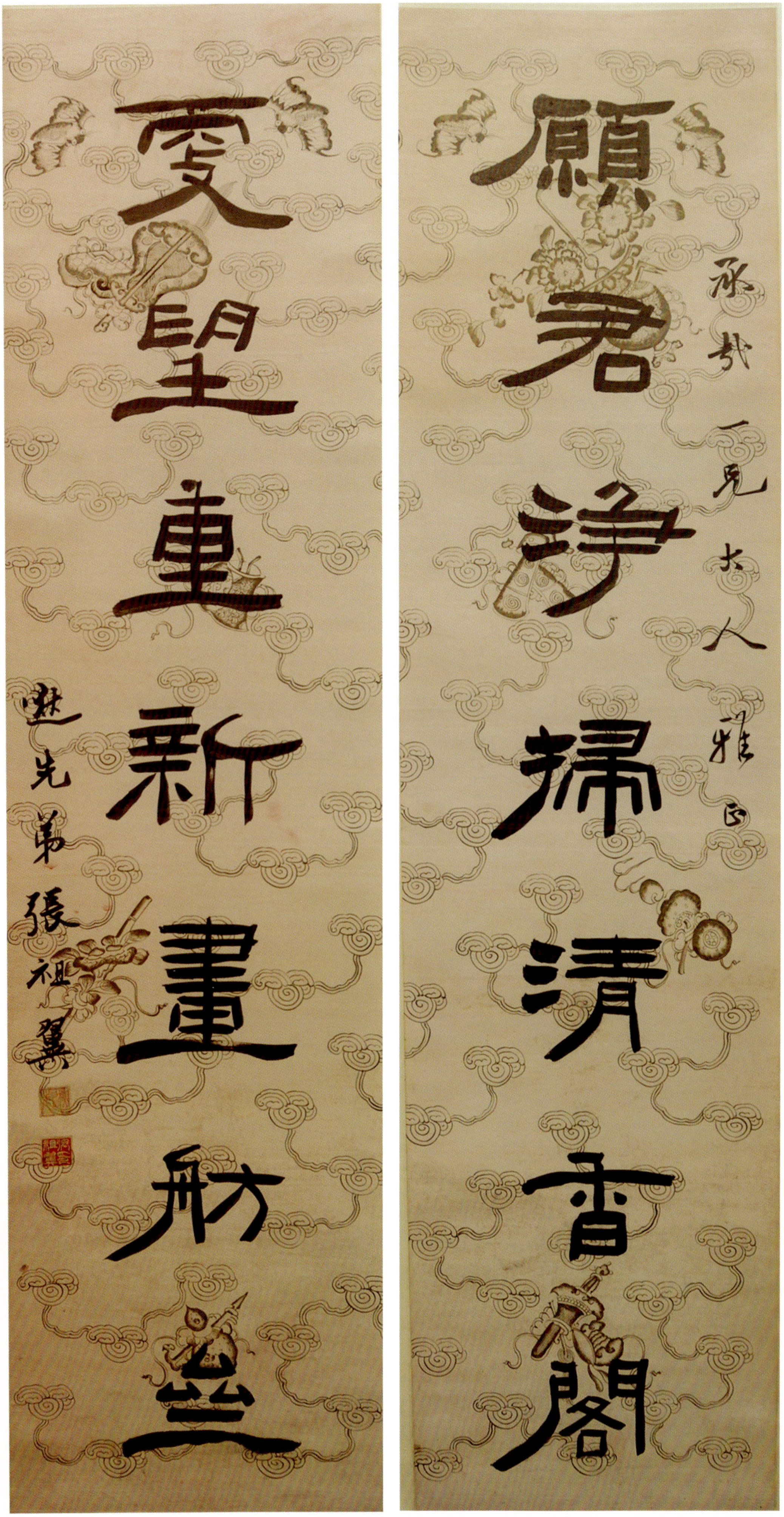

18. 隶书七言 联
Couplet of Seven Character Poem in Clerical Script

民国　张祖翼
Republic of China, Zhang Zuyi

纵 132 厘米　横 33 厘米

释文：愿君净扫清香阁
　　　更望重新画舫斋

张祖翼(1849—1917)，字逖先，又号磊庵，安徽桐城人。幼年即好篆、隶、金石之学，篆宗石鼓、钟鼎书，隶法汉碑，刻印师邓石如。亦工行、楷。其书法天骨开张，力韵具足。

19. 无量寿佛图 轴
Buddha of Infinite Life

民国　郑文焯
Republic of China,
Zheng Wenzhuo

纵 114.5 厘米　横 53.3 厘米

郑文焯(1856—1918),字小坡,号叔问,别号大鹤山人,内务府汉军正白旗人。濡染家学,工诗词,通医理,精金石考证之学,工书及篆刻。善画,山水高古,颇有华嵒骀宕神趣。花卉亦挥洒自如。亦善人物。其画风颇有徐渭余韵。

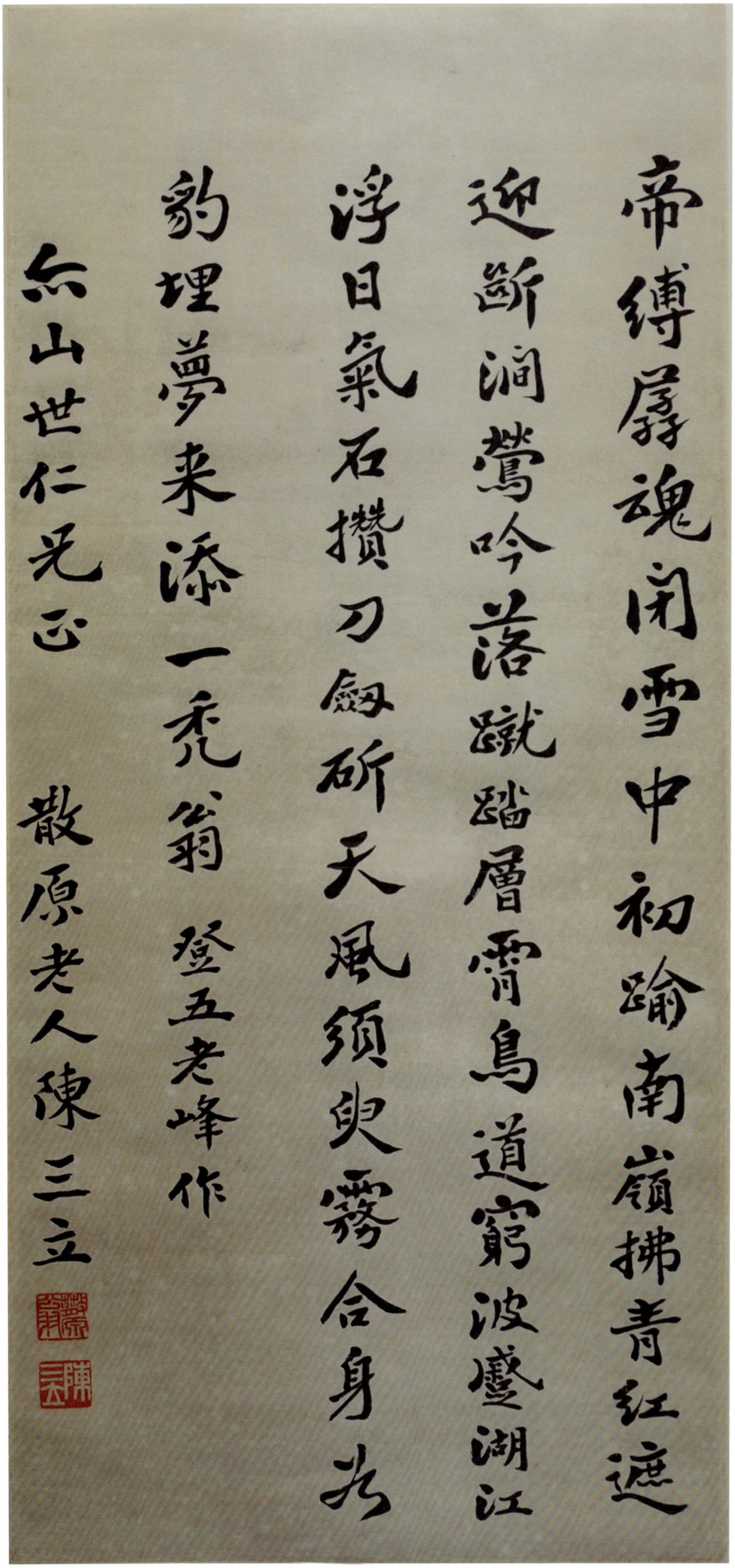

20. 行书七言 轴
Scroll of Seven Character Poem in Running Script

民国　陈三立
Republic of China, Chen Sanli

纵 81 厘米　横 35.7 厘米

释文：
帝缚孱魂闭雪中 初逾南岭拂青红
遮迎断涧莺吟落 蹴踏层霄鸟道穷
波蹙湖江浮日气 石攒刀剑斫天风
须臾雾合身如豹 埋梦来添一秃翁

陈三立(1856—1937)，字伯严，号散原，江西修水人。德业文章映照海内，诗学宋人，为近代名家。书法苍劲，自成矩范。

21. 荷塘鸳鸯图 轴
Painting of Mandarin Ducks on a Lotus Flower Pond

民国　　齐白石
Republic of China, Qi Baishi

纵 87.5 厘米　横 46.5 厘米

齐白石(1863—1957),小名阿芝,字萍生,号白石。湖南湘潭人。擅画花鸟虫鱼,笔墨纵横雄健,造型简练质朴,神态活泼,色彩鲜明强烈,为世界近代最有名的画家之一。此为齐白石早年之作。

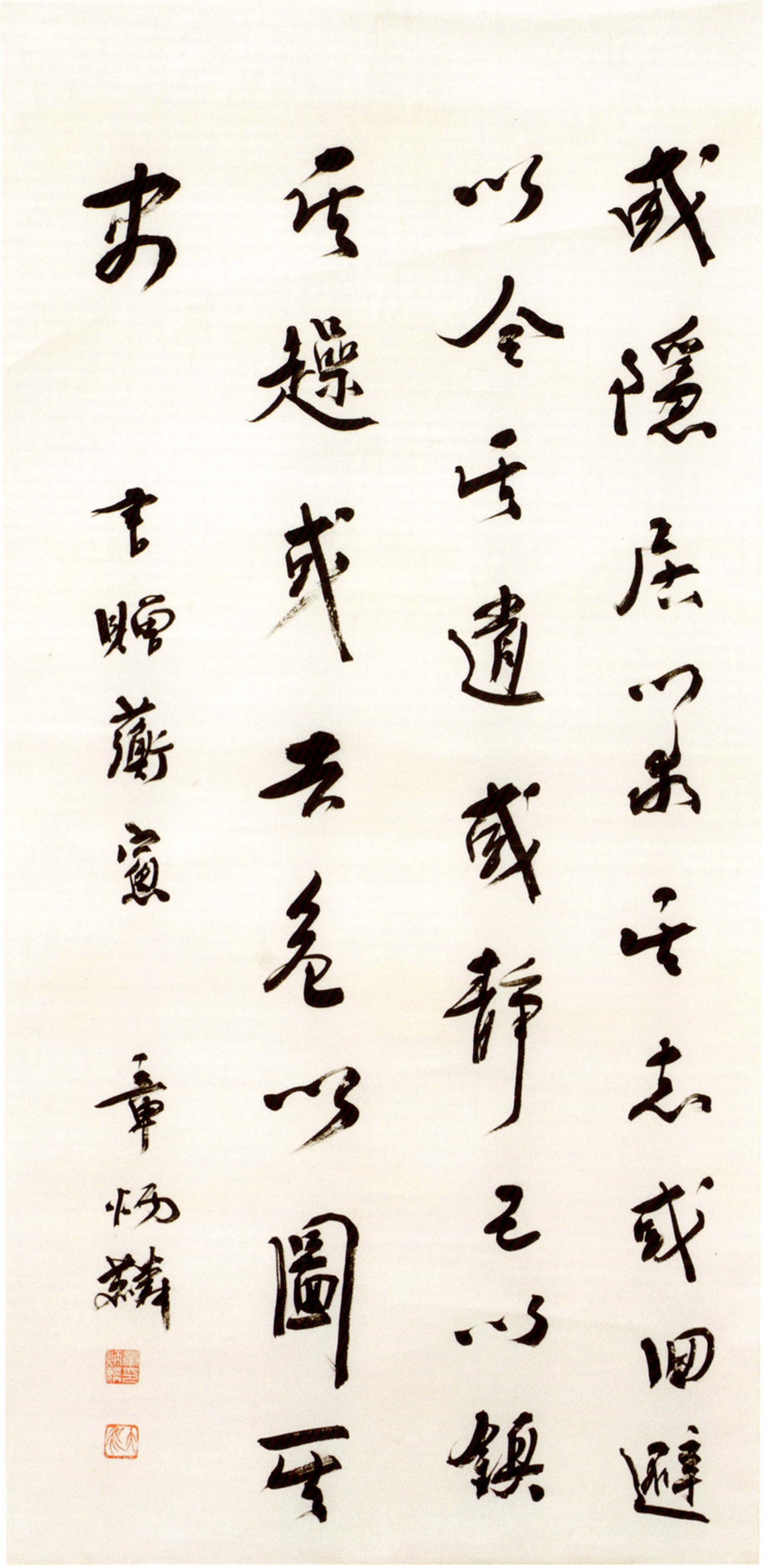

22. 行书七言 轴
Scroll of Seven Character
Poem in Running Style

民国　　章炳麟
Republic of China, Zhang Binglin

纵 98 厘米　横 48 厘米

释文：或隐居以求其志
　　　或回避以全其道
　　　或静己以镇其躁
　　　或去危以图其安

章炳麟(1868—1936)，原名绛，字枚叔，又字太炎。浙江余杭人。中国近代国学大师，著作丰富，有章氏丛书传世。工籀、篆，行书富金石气。

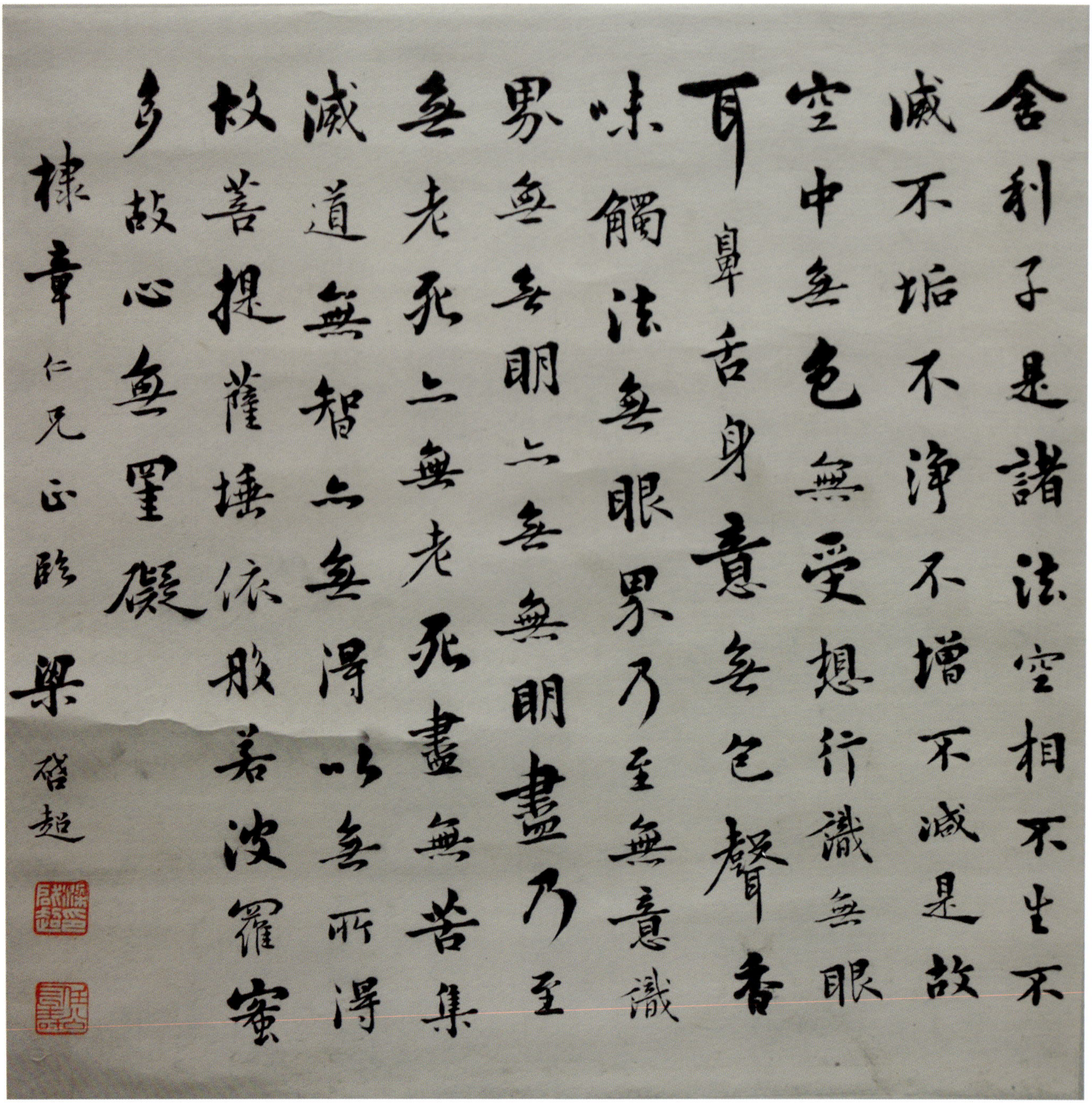

23. 行书佛经 轴

Sutra in Running Script

民国　　梁启超

Republic of China, Liang Qichao

纵 33 厘米　横 35 厘米

释文：舍利子 是诸法空相 不生不灭 不垢不净 不增不减 是故空中无色 无受想行识
无眼耳鼻舌身意 无色声香味触法 无眼界 乃至无意识界 无无明 亦无无明尽
乃至无老死 亦无老死尽 无苦集灭道 无智亦无得 以无所得故
菩提萨埵 依般若波罗蜜多故 心无挂碍

梁启超(1873—1928)，字卓如，号任公，别署中国之新民，广东新会人。其书法以欧阳询为启蒙，宗北魏张黑女墓志、隋龙藏寺碑，笔法浑厚，刚柔并济，结字严谨。

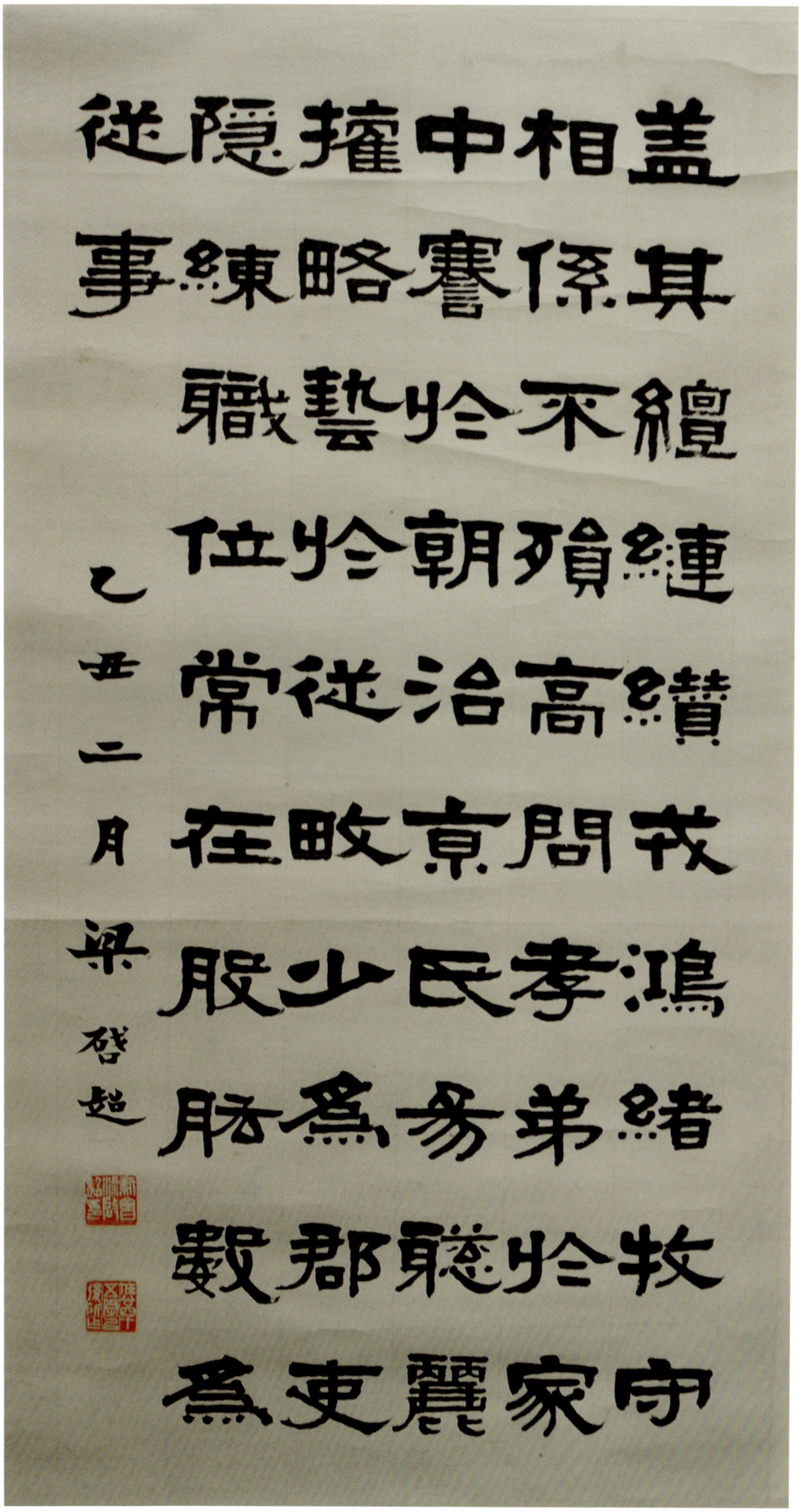

24. 隶书四言 轴
Scroll of Four Character Poem in Clerical Script

民国　　梁启超
Republic of China, Liang Qichao

纵 88 厘米　横 46 厘米

释文：盖其缠连 缵戎鸿绪
牧守相系 不殒高问
孝弟于家 中謇于朝
治京氏易 聪丽权略
艺于从畋 少为郡吏
隐练职位 常在股肱
数为从事

25. 松竹水仙图 轴

Painting of Pine Trees, Bamboos and Daffodils

民国　　经亨颐、张大千

Republic of China, Jing Hengyi, Zhang Daqian

纵 135 厘米　横 38.7 厘米

经亨颐(1875—1938),字子渊,号石禅,晚号颐渊。浙江上虞人。雅好治印、绘画,画从八大山人。其画以竹、松居多,寥寥几笔,疏落雅淡。

张大千(1899—1983),名权,后改作爰,号大千,小名季爰,四川内江人。其画气质高雅,所用墨彩精妙,于山水、花鸟、人物,无所不工。

26. 花卉图 轴
Vertical Painting Scroll of Flowers

民国　　陈衡恪
Republic of China, Chen Hengque

纵 132 厘米　横 33 厘米

陈衡恪(1876—1923),字师曾,号槐堂、朽者、朽道人。江西修水人。涂抹云烟,工诗文。画花卉挺拔俊逸,不取怪态,以习博物,故形态逼真。

27. 花卉图 轴
Vertical Painting Scroll of Flowers

民国　何香凝(画)、柳亚子(题字)
Republic of China, He Xiangning,
with an Inscription by Liu Yazi

纵 121.5 厘米　横 33.5 厘米

何香凝(1878—1972),女,原名瑞谏,又名谏,笔名双清楼主。广东南海人。擅作花鸟,偶作山水,笔致圆浑细腻,设色质朴。

柳亚子(1886—1958),原名慰高,字安如,别号亚子,江苏吴江人。清末,发起南社。以诗文驰名海内。书法狂草,自成一家。

28. 花鸟图 轴

Painting of Birds and Flowers

民国　　陈树人

Republic of China,Chen Shuren

纵 130 厘米　横 45 厘米

陈树人(1883—1948),原名政,以字行,别署猛进,晚号安定老人。广东番禺人。其绘画注重写生,摒弃仿古,花卉赋色,别有技巧。

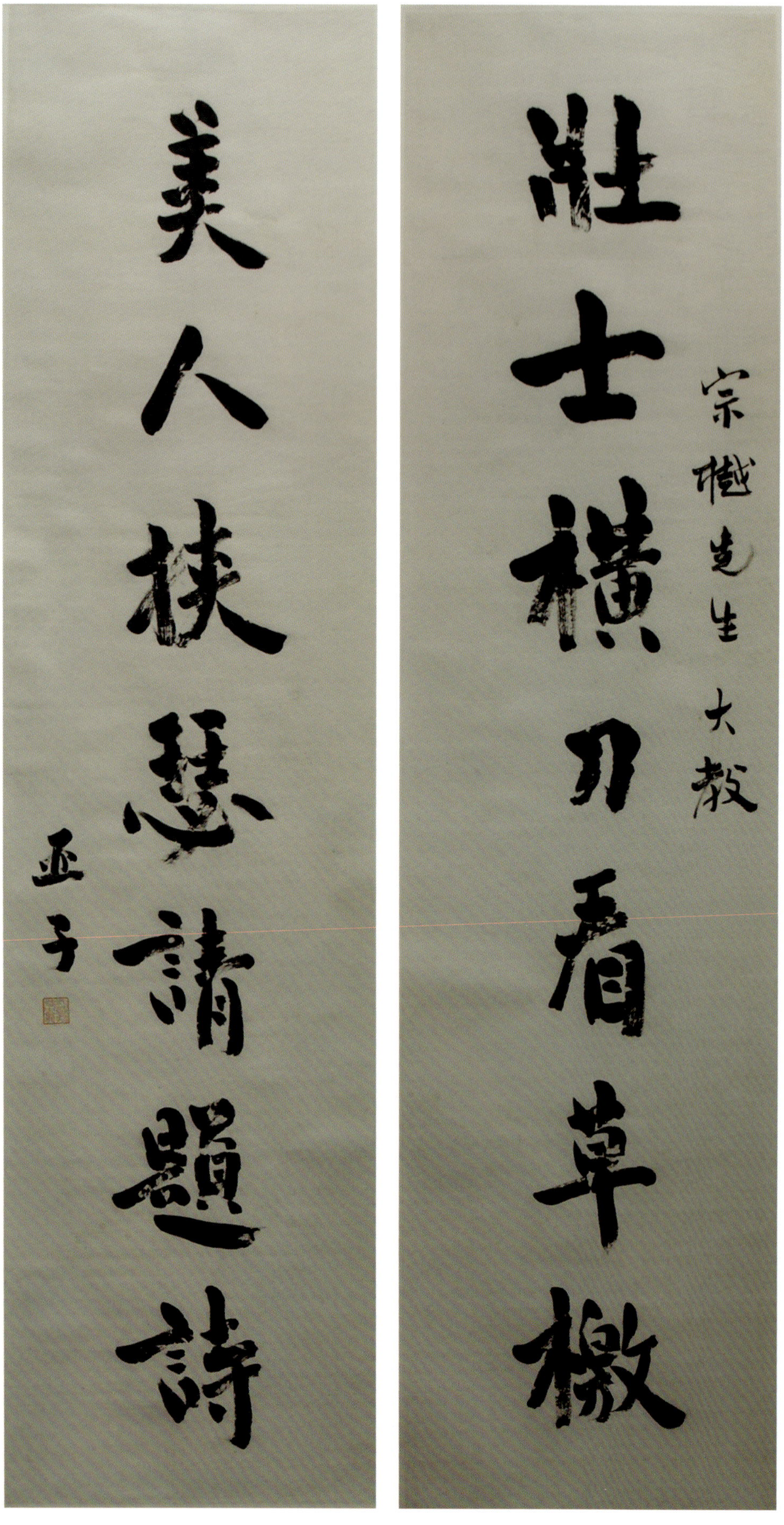

29. 行书七言 联
Couplet of Seven Character Poem in Running Script

民国　　柳亚子
Republic of China,Liu Yazi

纵 134 厘米　横 33.2 厘米

释文：壮士横刀看草檄
　　　美人扶瑟请题诗

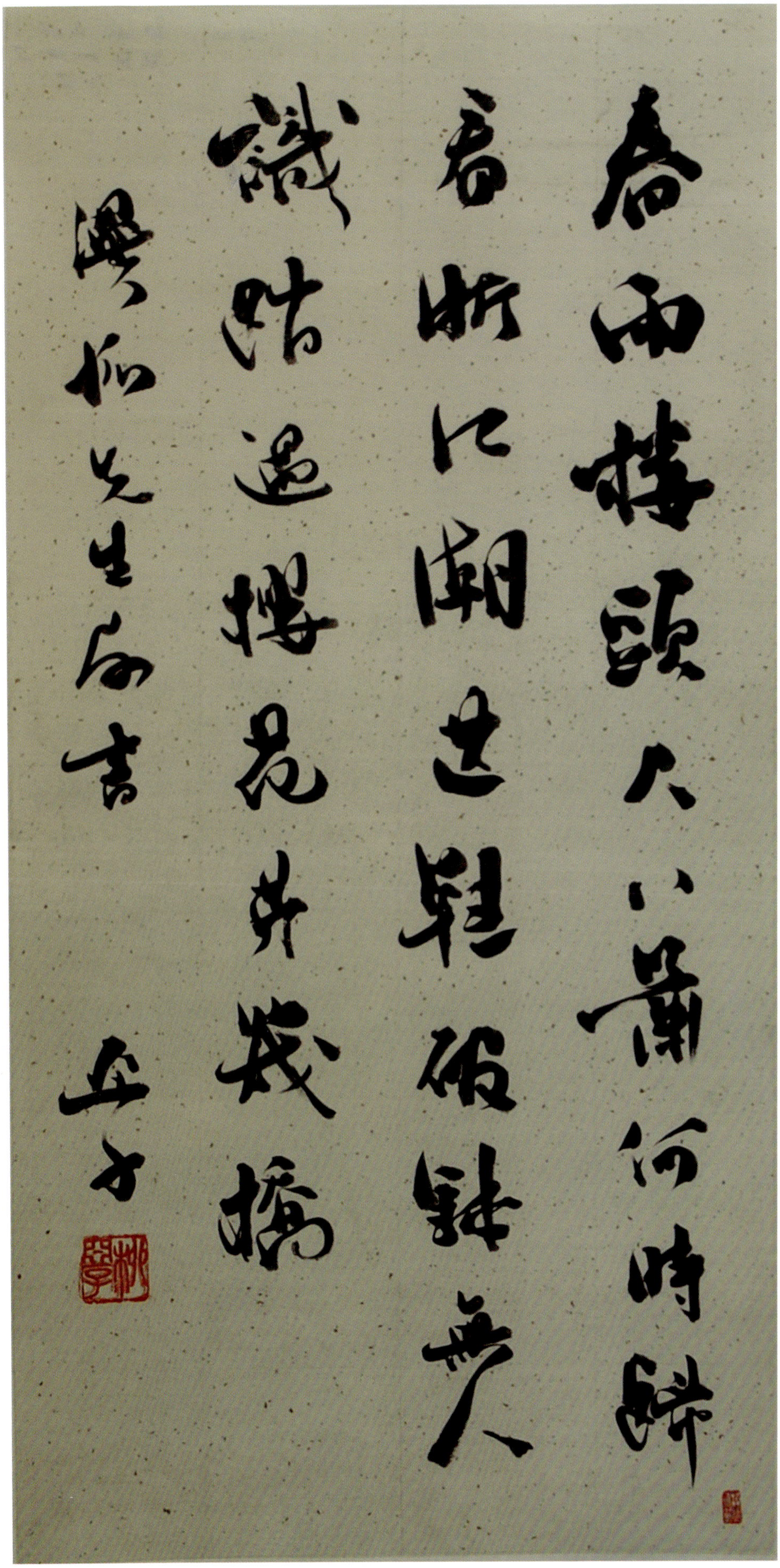

30. 行书七言 轴
Scroll of Seven Character Poem in Running Script

民国　　柳亚子
Republic of China, Liu Yazi

纵 64.2 厘米　横 31.8 厘米

释文：春雨楼头尺八箫
　　　何时归看浙江潮
　　　芒鞋破钵无人识
　　　踏过樱花第几桥

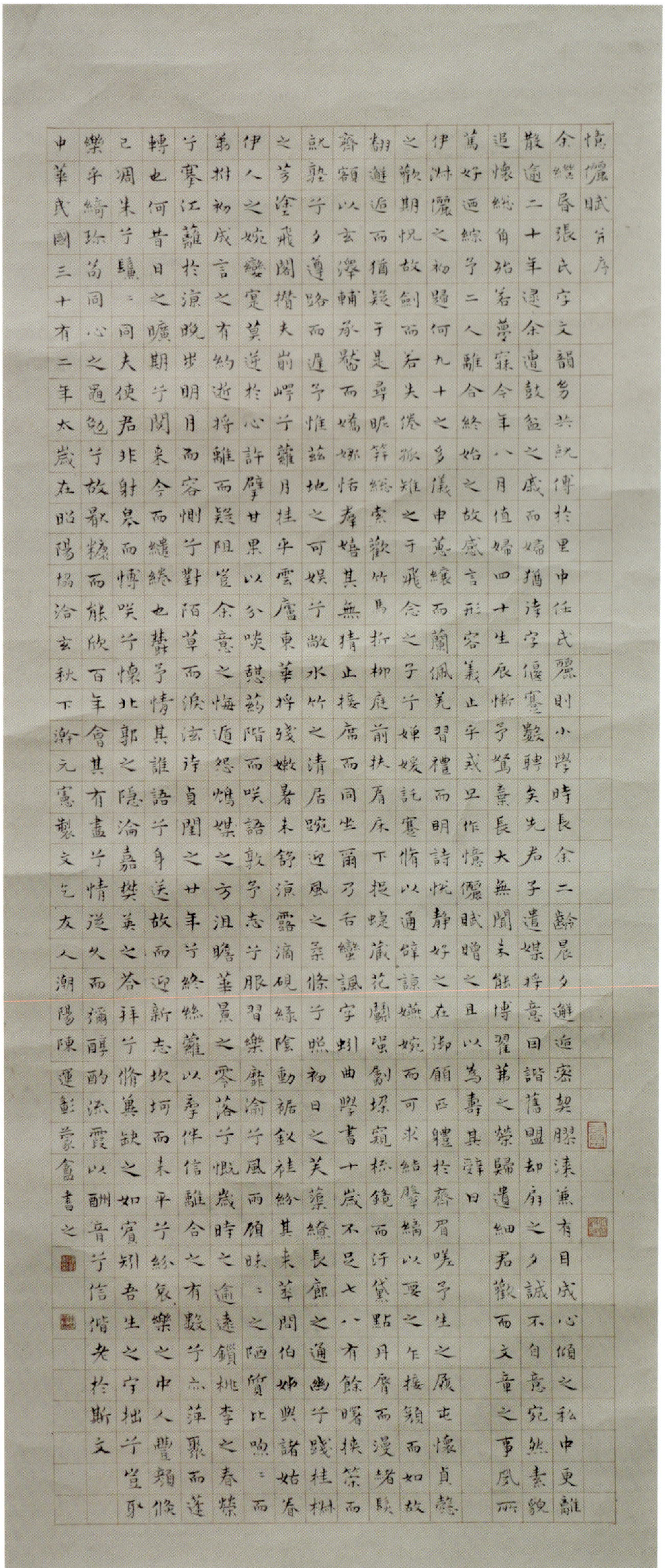

31. 忆丽赋并序 轴
Verse of Yi Li and the Preface

民国　　陈运彰
Republic of China, Chen Yunzhang

纵 65.2 厘米　横 27.6 厘米

陈运彰(1905—1956),字君谟,一字蒙安,广东潮阳铜盂人。书法笔画圆润,流转秀逸,字体娟秀,行间宽疏,温文尔雅,颇有宋四家的风格。

32. 赤玉盛开图 横幅
Horizontal Scroll of Cherry-apple in Full Bloom

现代　王个簃
People's Republic of China,Wang Geyi

纵 67 厘米　横 135 厘米

王个簃(1897—1988),名贤,字启之,江苏海门人。笃好诗文、金石、书画。师吴昌硕,学书画篆刻。擅长写意花卉,以篆籀之笔入画,用笔浑厚刚健,笔势静蕴含蓄。

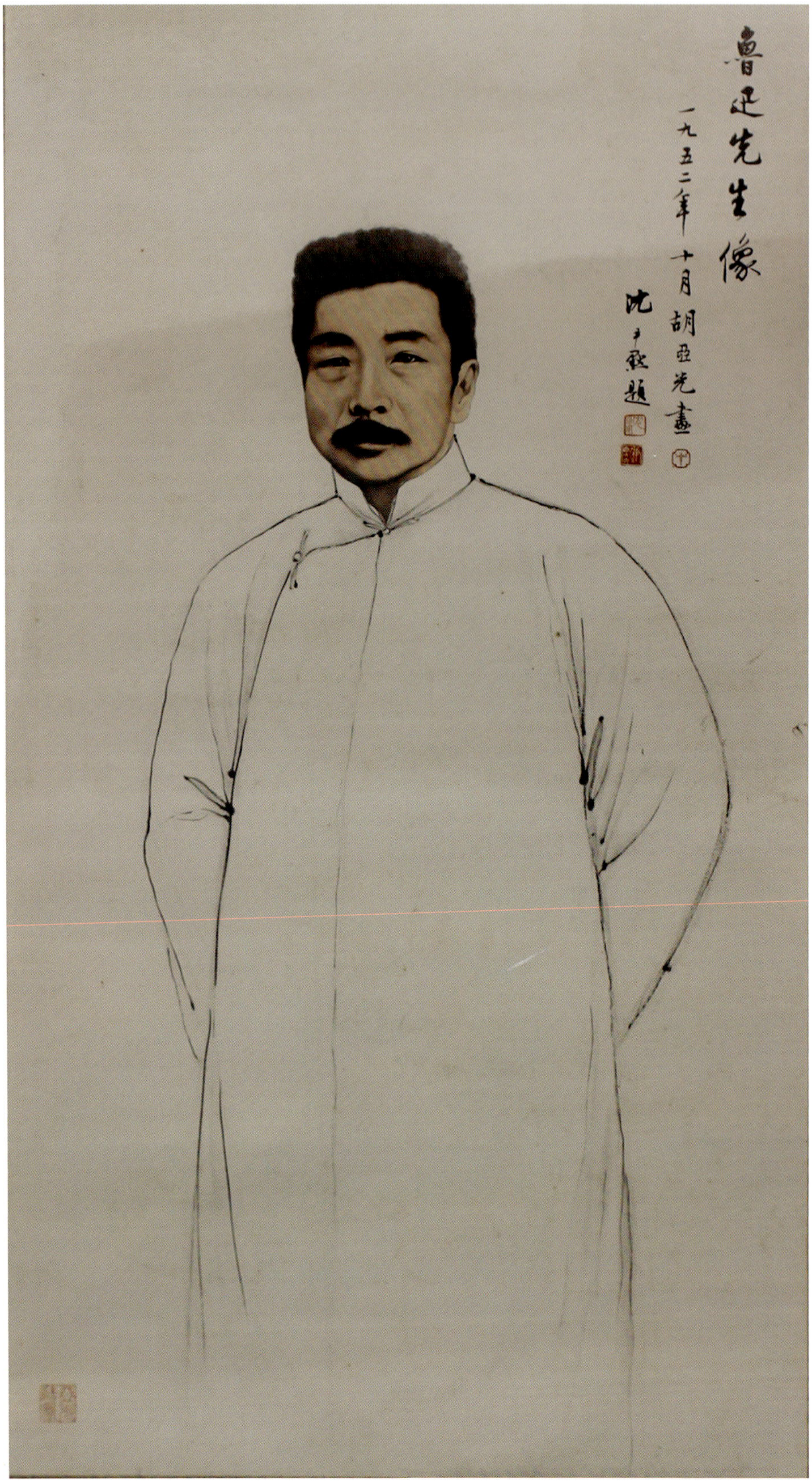

33. 鲁迅先生像 轴
Vertical Scroll Portrait of Mr. Lu Xun

现代　胡亚光(画)、沈尹默(题字)
People's Republic of China, Hu Yaguang, with an Inscription by Shen Yinmo

纵 109 厘米　横 61 厘米

胡亚光(1901—1986),名文球,字亚光,号梦蝶楼主,又号安定居士,浙江杭州人。擅人物写照,雅韵欲流、神态酣足。

沈尹默(1883—1971),原名君默,字中、秋明,号君墨,浙江吴兴人。书法用笔挥洒自如,如行云流水。笔墨跌宕起伏,浓淡相间,有欧阳修之神韵,带赵孟頫之骨肌。

34. 嵩寿图 横幅

Horizontal Scroll Painting of Longevity

现代　　谢孝思、吴羖木、张辛稼

People's Republic of China, Xie Xiaosi, Wu Yangmu, Zhang Xinjia

纵 96 厘米　横 177 厘米

谢孝思(1905—2008),字仲谋,贵州贵阳人。善于在画面上将诗情画意融为一体,加上清新隽永的题款,紧扣题旨,使整个画面浑然一体,显现出浓郁的民族特色。
吴羖木(1921—2009),名彭,号小铜,浙江石门人。用笔柔韧刚劲,用墨浓淡相宜,构图留虚空,设色妍雅,意境清丽。
张辛稼(1909—1991),字星阶,别署霜屋老农,江苏苏州人。书画皆精。用笔苍劲,设色明丽,意境清新,风格独特。

35. 仕女图 轴
Painting of a Maid

现代　　陈小翠
People's Republic of China,
Chen Xiaocui

纵 98 厘米　横 46.4 厘米

陈小翠(1907—1968),女,又名玉翠、翠娜,浙江杭县人。师从杨士猷、冯超然学画。擅长工笔仕女、花卉画。画风清雅俊逸,饶有风姿。

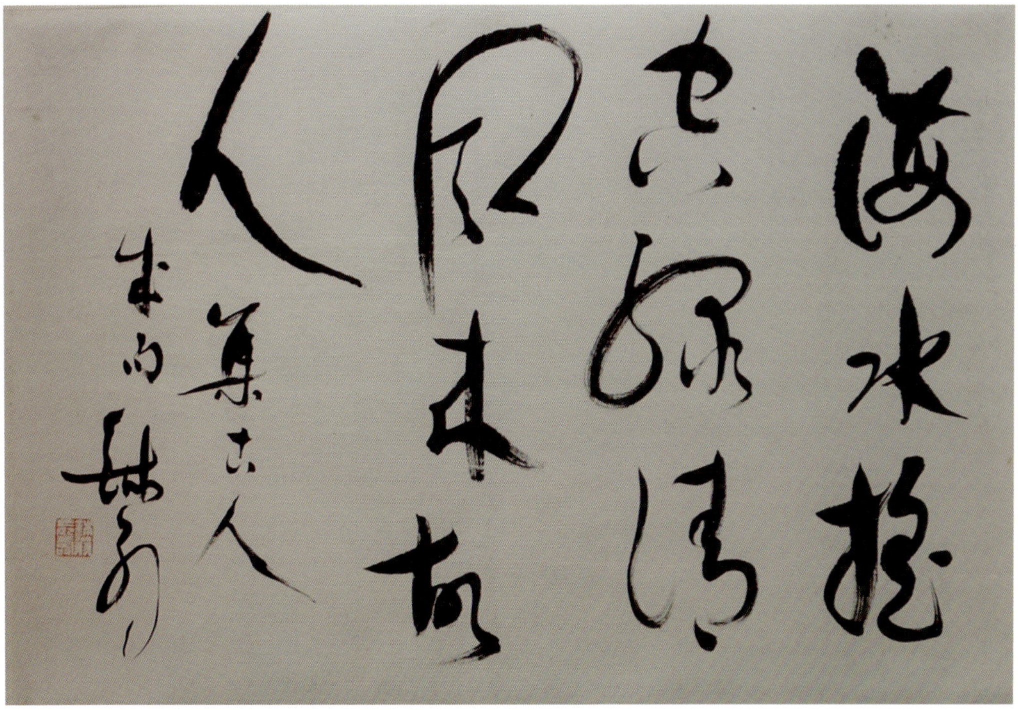

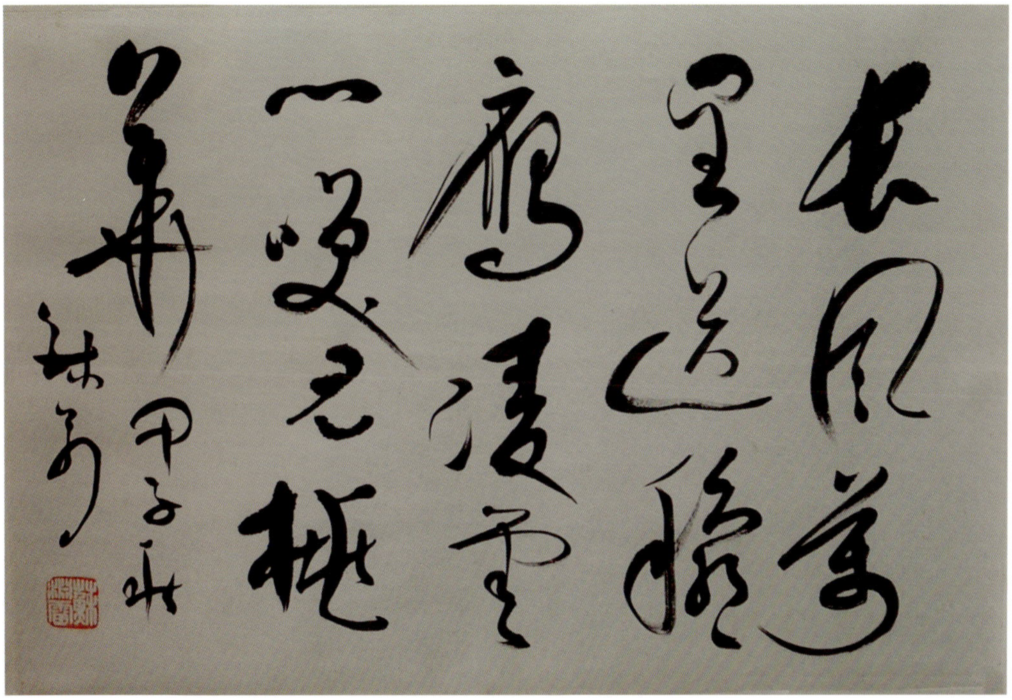

36. 草书二幅 册页
Two Pieces of Calligraphy in Cursive Script

现代　苏渊雷
People's Republic of China, Su Yuanlei

纵 33.3 厘米　横 51 厘米

释文：海水摇空绿 清风来故人
　　　长风万里送秋雁 凌云一笑见桃花

苏渊雷(1908—1995),原名中常,字仲翔,晚号钵翁,又号遁园。浙江苍南人。雅好文艺,兼擅书画,笔墨洒脱,逸笔草草。

37. 斗雪迎春图 横幅
Spring Snow Painting

现代　　张辛稼
People's Republic of China,Zhang Xinjia

纵 63 厘米　横 99.5 厘米

38. 鸬鹚图 横幅
Horizontal Scroll Painting of Cormorants

现代　　唐云
People's Republic of China,Tang Yun

纵 66.5 厘米　横 135 厘米

唐云(1910—1993),字侠尘,别号药城、大石翁。浙江杭州人。其画大胆落墨,细心收拾,笔墨融北派厚重与南派超逸于一体。

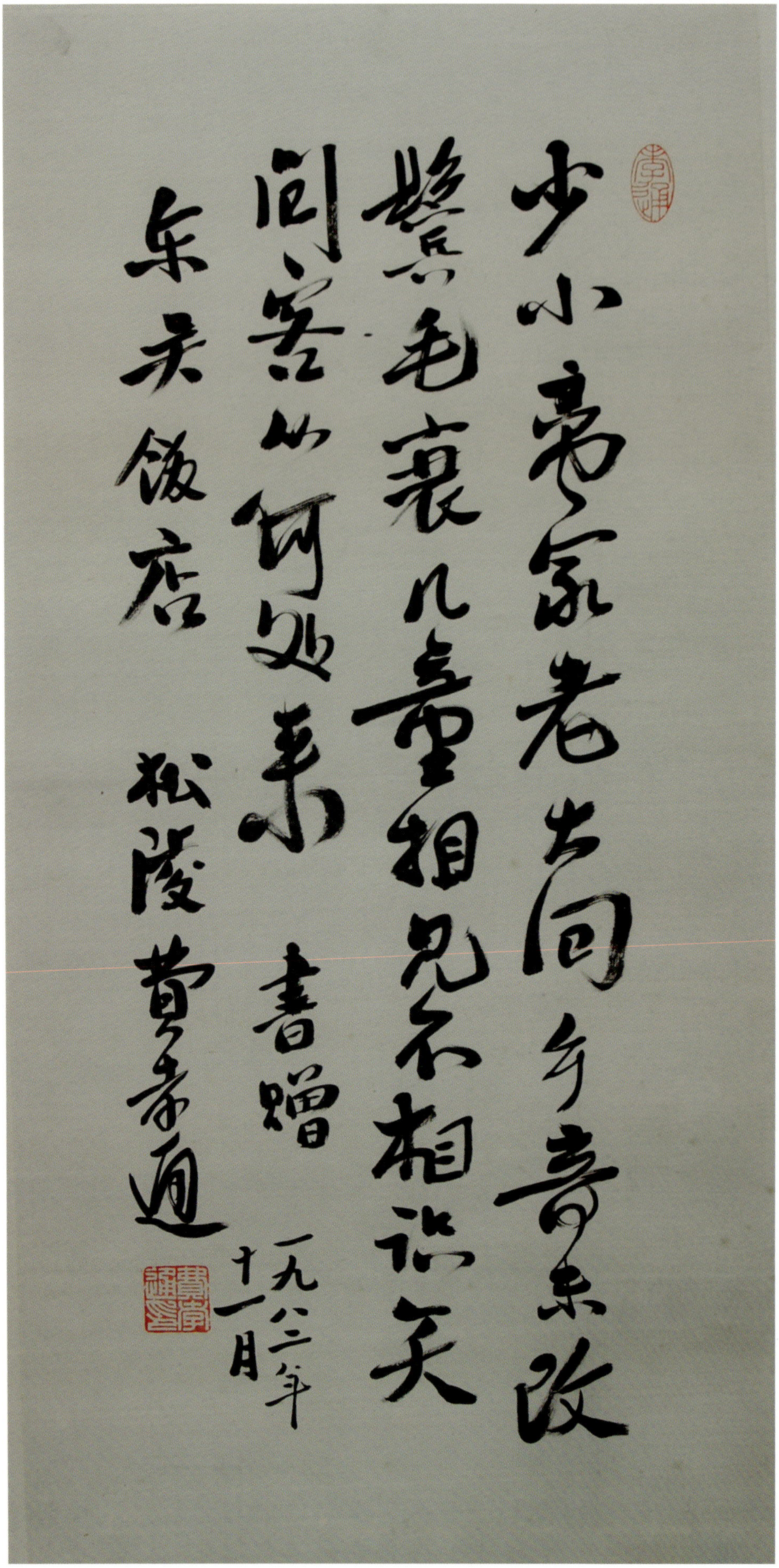

39. 行书七言 轴

Scroll of Seven Character Poem in Running Script

现代　　费孝通

People's Republic of China, Fei Xiaotong

纵 69 厘米　横 34.5 厘米

释文：少小离家老大回
　　　乡音未改鬓毛衰
　　　儿童相见不相识
　　　笑问客从何处来

费孝通(1910—2005)，祖籍江苏吴江，全国人大原副委员长、著名社会学家、人类学家、社会活动家，中国社会学和人类学的奠基人。

40. 汉柏图 轴
Vertical Panting of Chinese Cypress

现代　　徐子鹤
People's Republic of China,Xu Zihe

纵 76 厘米　横 51 厘米

徐子鹤(1916—1999),字翼,江苏苏州人。善画梅、写竹,更以十上黄山、善画黄山而著称。笔墨源于南宋四家,淳雅流畅,清丽洒脱。

41. 太湖春色图 斗方
Painting of Spring on the Taihu Lake

现代　宋文治
People's Republic of China, Song Wenzhi

纵 66 厘米　横 66 厘米

宋文治(1919—1999),江苏太仓人。其山水画笔墨融洽南北,骨力劲健,气势高迈,虽善作高远之景,却又喜绘江南三月,风光旖旎,另具婀都之姿。

42. 庭园小趣图 轴
Fun in the Courtyard

现代　杜重划
People's Republic of China,
Du Chonghua

纵 96 厘米　横 43 厘米

杜重划(1920—1990)，四川眉山人。擅长中国画。任教于苏南文化教育学院艺术系、江苏师范学院国画系、苏州美术专科学校、南京师范学院美术系。苏州国画院专职画家。

43. 松竹梅图 轴
Painting of Pine Bamboo Plum

现代　吴敉木、崔护、张辛稼
People's Republic of China, Wu Yangmu, Cui Hu, Zhang Xinjia

纵 135 厘米　横 67 厘米

崔护（1924—2008），江苏苏州人。特好写竹，为一大特色。作品清新隽逸、生动洒脱。

44. 武夷山图 轴
Vertical Painting of Mount Wuyi

现代　　姚　奎
People's Republic of China, Yao Kui

纵 68 厘米　横 44 厘米

姚奎(1936—2007),山西垣曲人。擅画山水,不为成法所囿,致力创新。其作品重装饰情趣,厚重饱满,意境别具,个性鲜明。

石器

Stoneware

1. 穿孔石斧(上)、石镰(右中)、石钺(左下)、石凿(右下)　新石器时代
Perforated Axes, Stone Sickle, Perforated Zax, Stone Chisel, The Neolithic Age

2. 石纺轮　新石器时代
Stone Spinning Wheel, The Neolithic Age

陶瓷器

Pottery and Porcelain

1. 陶拍(上)、陶垫(中)、陶纺轮(下)
新石器时代
Pottery Bat, Pottery Pad, Pottery Spinning Wheel, The Neolithic Age

2. 陶罐　新石器时代
Pottery Pot, The Neolithic Age

3. 屋顶形器盖陶罐　新石器时代
Pottery Jar with Roof-shaped Cover, The Neolithic Age

4. 双大耳红陶罐　新石器时代
Red Pottery Pot with Double Big Handles, The Neolithic Age

5. 网格印纹陶罐　西周
Mesh-Checked Pottery Pot,The Western Zhou Dynasty

6. 网格印纹陶罐　春秋
Mesh-Checked Pottery Pot, The Spring and Autumn Period

7. 黑皮陶罐 战国
Black Pottery Crock, The Warring States

8. 灰陶鼎　战国
Grey Pottery Tripod, The Warring States

9. 原始瓷甬钟 战国
Protoporcelain Bells, The Warring States

瓷器是中国的重大发明,早在商代就出现了原始瓷器,原始瓷器的出现是制陶工艺高度发展的结果。春秋战国之际以越国为中心的原始瓷器工艺发展到巅峰,其中以原始瓷甬钟为代表,是仿铜甬钟而制作的。据说越王勾践禁用铜制作礼器,因此用原始瓷仿铜礼器。环太湖地区一带是原始甬钟集中出土的地区,陶质坚硬、印纹精美的原始瓷仿铜礼器是古越人特有的陶瓷工艺。无锡鸿山越国贵族墓出土器物为江浙一带越国贵族墓之最,其中有原始瓷甬钟 26 件,可惜大部分已碎裂。

苏州大学博物馆征集的战国初期的一套原始瓷甬钟,自大渐小共 9 件,是国内迄今为止发现的保存完好数量较多的成套原始瓷甬钟,敲击时有清亮悦耳的声音。钟有上细下粗的甬,上有刻划纹。左右篆部各有 9 个枚,篆部和舞部有细密的弧线戳印纹,制作精美。这套原始瓷甬钟出土于水坑,上面的青釉由于长期浸泡而脱落,但残存的青釉仍依稀可辨,为原始瓷器中不可多得的珍品。

10. 茧形灰陶壶 西汉
Cocoon-shaped Grey Pottery Kettle, The Western Han Dynasty

11. 双大耳灰陶罐　西汉
Grey Pottery Vessel with Double Big Handles, The Western Han Dynasty

12. 釉陶罐(一) 汉代
Glazed Pottery Pot(Ⅰ),Han Dynasty

13. 釉陶罐(二) 汉代
Glazed Pottery Pot(Ⅱ),Han Dynasty

14. 陶谷仓 汉代
Pottery Barn, Han Dynasty

15. 陶奁 汉代
Pottery Casket, Han Dynasty

16. 釉陶壶　汉代
Glazed Pottery Pot, Han Dynasty

17. 绿釉陶勺　汉代
Green-glazed Pottery Spoon, Han Dynasty

18. 陶井　汉代
Pottery Well, Han Dynasty

汉代厚葬之风尤甚。西汉中期以后，增添了各种专门为随葬而烧造的陶质明器，包括仓、灶、井、磨、楼阁模型和猪、狗、鸡、鸭等禽畜偶像。

19.“长乐未央”瓦当 汉代
Eaves Tiles with Epigraph“Endless Joy”, Han Dynasty

20. 云气纹瓦当 汉代
Eaves Tiles with a Design of Clouds, Han Dynasty

21. 陶屋 汉代
Pottery House, Han Dynasty

22. 青釉立鸟瓷盅　西晋
Green-glazed Porcelain Bowl with a Design of a Standing Bird, The Western Jin Dynasty

23. 斜方格纹四系青瓷盂　西晋
Slanting-mesh-pattern Celadon Jar with Four Handles,
The Western Jin Dynasty

24. 双肩耳瓷罐　西晋
Porcelain Pot with Double Handles, The Western Jin Dynasty

2009 年苏州东山镇岭下村古瓷窑遗址出土
Unearthed from ruins of ancient kiln in Lingxia village, Dongshan town, Suzhou in 2009.

25. 青釉四系耳瓷罐　东晋
Green-glazed Porcelain Jar with Four Handles,
The Eastern Jin Dynasty

2009年苏州东山镇岭下村古瓷窑遗址出土
Unearthed from ruins of ancient kiln in Lingxia village, Dongshan town, Suzhou in 2009.

26. 青釉瓷钵　东晋
Green-glazed Porcelain Alms Bowl, The Eastern Jin Dynasty

2009年苏州东山镇岭下村古瓷窑遗址出土
Unearthed from ruins of ancient kiln in Lingxia village, Dongshan town, Suzhou in 2009.

27. 四系青瓷罐 东晋
Celadon Pot with Four Handles, The Eastern Jin Dynasty

28. 青瓷盘 东晋
Celadon Plate, The Eastern Jin Dynasty

29. 瓦当　南朝
Eaves Tiles, Southern Dynasty

30. 四系青瓷壶　隋代
Celadon Kettle with Four Handles, Sui Dynasty

隋代青瓷是在南北朝时期陶瓷生产的基础上发展起来的。盘口壶是东汉至唐代流行的一种盛具，贮水或贮酒用，是中国古青瓷的代表器。隋代壶体瘦长，盘口高而微撇，颈长且直，腹呈椭圆形、条状系等。此器物腹部以上安装四系，底部有支烧痕迹。灰白色胎质地坚硬，豆绿色釉施遍器身，造型匀称。

31. 四系青瓷罐 隋代
Celadon Pot with Four Handles,Sui Dynasty

32. 青瓷盅　隋代
Celadon Wine-cup, Sui Dynasty

33. 双系青瓷执壶　唐代
Celadon Ewer with Double Handles, Tang Dynasty

执壶又称“注子”、“注壶”，隋代出现的酒具。唐前期器呈盘口，短颈，鼓腹，圆筒形或六角形，短直流，曲柄，壶体较矮，假圈足。唐中晚期大量流行，基本取代了鸡首壶、凤首壶等。这时期执壶式样繁多，有短流、长流、曲柄、直柄等数种。

34. 越窑青瓷盆 唐代
Yue Kiln Celadon Pot, Tang Dynasty

35. 花瓣形青瓷水盂　五代
Petal-patterned Celadon Water-jar, The Five Dynasties

36. 邢窑白瓷小碗　五代
Xing Kiln White Porcelain Bowl, The Five Dynasties

37. 莲花刻纹瓷诸葛碗 宋代
Zhu-Ge Porcelain Bowl with a Design of Lotus, Song Dynasty

38. 酱褐釉双耳瓷壶　宋代
Black-brown-glazed Pottery Kettle with Double Handles, Song Dynasty

39. 酱褐釉陶壶　宋代
Black-brown-glazed Porcelain Kettle, Song Dynasty

40. 孔雀蓝釉梅瓶　宋代
Peacock-blue-glazed Vase, Song Dynasty

41. 影青瓷碗 宋代
Shadowy Blue Porcelain Bowl, Song Dynasty

42. 影青暗花葵口瓷碗　宋代
Shadowy Blue Sunflower-shaped Porcelain Bowl, Song Dynasty

43. 影青瓷魂瓶 南宋
Shadowy Blue Porcelain Vase, The Southern Song Dynasty

44. 湖田窑影青暗花双鱼瓷碗　南宋
Double-fish-patterned Shadowy Blue Porcelain Bowl from Hu Tian Kiln, The Southern Song Dynasty

45. 银扣刻花云龙纹盘　南宋
Porcelain Plate with a Design of Dragon,The Southern Song Dynasty

46. 钧窑小瓷碟 金代
Jun Kiln Small Porcelain Dish, Jin Dynasty

47. 影青刻花瓷碗　元代
Celadon Porcelain Bowl with a Design of Flower,Yuan Dynasty

48. 钧窑瓷碗　元代
Jun Kiln Porcelain Bowl, Yuan Dynasty

49. 龙泉窑高足碗 元代
Long Quan Kiln Porcelain Bowl with High Bottom,Yuan Dynasty

50. 龙泉窑小瓷盘 元代
Long Quan Kiln Small Porcelain Dish, Yuan Dynasty

51. 龙泉窑高圈足瓷碗　明代
Long Quan Kiln Porcelain Bowl with High Bottom, Ming Dynasty

52. 龙泉窑印花人物瓷碗(一) 明代
Long Quan Kiln Porcelain Bowl with a Figure Design(Ⅰ),Ming Dynasty

53. 龙泉窑印花人物瓷碗(二) 明代
Long Quan Kiln Porcelain Bowl with a Figure Design(Ⅱ),Ming Dynasty

此碗器型工整,无论是胎、色、釉,都是浙江龙泉窑烧造;发色好,釉色肥厚亮泽,手感温润如玉;碗内印有人物。

54. 白瓷瓶　明代
White-porcelain Vase, Ming Dynasty

55. 青花五彩人物盆底插屏　明代
Five-color-glazed Figure-stamped Celadon Bottle,Ming Dynasty

56. 德化窑暗花碗　明代
De Hua Kiln Porcelain Bowl, Ming Dynasty

57. 青花瓷碗 明代
Stamped Blue-and-white Porcelain Bowl, Ming Dynasty

58. 青花花卉纹瓷碗 明代
Stamped Celadon Bowl with a Pattern of Flowers, Ming Dynasty

59. 青花人物纹瓷碗　明代
Stamped Celadon Bowl with a Figure Pattern, Ming Dynasty

60. 青花瓷汤匙 明代
Stamped Blue-and-white Porcelain Spoon, Ming Dynasty

61. 青花瓷罐 明代
Stamped Blue-and-white Porcelain Pot,Ming Dynasty

62. 三彩小罐 明代
Three-color Pot, Ming Dynasty

63. 琉璃云龙纹瓦当　明代
Color-glazed Eaves Tile with a Design of Dragon, Ming Dynasty

64. 琉璃龙纹瓦当(一) 明代
Color-glazed Eaves Tile with a Design of Dragon(Ⅰ),Ming Dynasty

65. 琉璃龙纹瓦当(二) 明代
Color-glazed Eaves Tile with a Design of Dragon(Ⅱ), Ming Dynasty

66. 磁州窑瓷寿星像 明代
Porcelain God of Longevity from Ci Zhou Kiln,
Ming Dynasty

67. 五彩瓷盘 清代顺治年间
Five-color-glazed Porcelain Plate,
Shunzhi's Reign of Qing Dynasty

彩瓷是成熟于明代的釉上彩绘瓷，也称“大明五彩”。由于工艺技法和使用材料的原因，在清代康熙年间亦称为“硬彩”。五彩瓷的制作，是以烧制好的白釉器为基础，生料、矾红勾线，只有矾红深浅洗色，其他均以透明色平填。描绘图案纹样后入窑烧烤，经 750℃至 850℃窑火烧烤而成。色彩以红、绿、黄、蓝、紫、孔雀绿等色多见，有的还加饰金彩。

68. 豇豆红瓷盘　清代雍正年间
Cowpea Red Porcelain Dish,
Yongzheng's Reign of Qing Dynasty

豇豆红是铜红高温釉中的一种，为清代康熙晚期出现的铜红釉品种。因其色调淡雅宜人,以不均匀的粉红色、犹如红豇豆一般、造型轻灵秀美而得名。豇豆红釉质都很匀净细腻,含有粉质。豇豆红无大器,常见为文房用具,如太白尊(水盂)、石榴尊、菊瓣瓶、柳叶瓶、洗、印盒等。

69. 青花瓷盘　清代雍正年间
Stamped Celadon Bowl, Yongzheng's Reign of Qing Dynasty

70. 豇豆红瓷盘 清代乾隆年间
Cowpea-red Porcelain Dish,
Qianlong's Reign of Qing Dynasty

71. 茶叶末瓷瓶 清代
Tea-dust Glazed Porcelain Bottle, Qing Dynasty

72. 祭红瓷瓶　清代
Red Porcelain Vase, Qing Dynasty

73. 石榴红瓷盂　清代
Garnet Porcelain Jar, Qing Dynasty

74. 斗彩瓷碟　清代
Polychrome Porcelain Dish, Qing Dynasty

75. 青釉瓷花瓶　清代
Blue-glazed Porcelain Vase, Qing Dynasty

76. 青花瓷罐　清代
Blue-and-white Porcelain Jar, Qing Dynasty

77. 瓷塑 清代
Porcelain Figurine, Qing Dynasty

78. 德化窑三足炉　清代
Three-legged Censer from De Hua Kiln, Qing Dynasty

79. 白瓷三足炉　清代
Three-legged White Porcelain Censer, Qing Dynasty

80. 建窑瓷马蹄杯　清代
Horseshoe Porcelain Cup from Jian Kiln, Qing Dynasty

81. 瓷花瓶　清代同治年间
Porcelain Vase, Tongzhi's Reign of Qing Dynasty

82. 蓝双兽耳琮式瓷瓶　清代光绪年间
Porcelain Vase with Double Beast-handles,
Guangxu's Reign of Qing Dynasty

83. 蟠龙纹瓷坛　清代光绪年间
Porcelain Jug with a Design of Dragon,
Guangxu's Reign of Qing Dynasty

俑

俑

Figurine

Figurine

1. 陶鸡　汉代
Pottery Chicken, Han Dynasty

2. 陶猪　汉代
Pottery Swine, Han Dynasty

3. 陶马头　汉代
Pottery Horse Head, Han Dynasty

4. 彩绘武士陶俑(一)　北魏
Polychrome Warrior Pottery Figurine(Ⅰ),The Northern Wei Dynasty

5. 彩绘武士陶俑(二)　北魏
Polychrome Warrior Pottery Figurine(Ⅱ),The Northern Wei Dynasty

6. 陶马(一)　北魏
Pottery Horse(Ⅰ),The Northern Wei Dynasty

7. 陶马(二) 北魏
Pottery Horse(Ⅱ),The Northern Wei Dynasty

8. 陶骆驼　北魏
Pottery Camel,The Northern Wei Dynasty

9. 陶镇墓兽　北魏
Pottery Tomb Beast, The Northern Wei Dynasty

10. 彩绘戴风帽陶俑　北魏
Polychrome Capped Pottery Figurine,
The Northern Wei Dynasty

11. 武士陶俑　北朝
Warrior Pottery Figurine, Northern Dynasty

12. 釉陶女俑　隋代
Color-glazed Maid Pottery Figurine, Sui Dynasty

13. 陶俑　隋代
Pottery Figurine, Sui Dynasty

14. 彩绘文官陶俑　唐代
Polychrome Pottery Figurine of Civil Official,
Tang Dynasty

俑的使用是为了使死者能在冥世继续如生前一样生活，所以，俑真实地负载了古代社会的各种信息，对研究古代的舆服制度、军阵排布、生活方式乃至中西文化交流皆有重要的意义，为我们勾勒出古代雕塑艺术发展的脉络以及历代审美习尚变迁的轨迹，成为了解中国古代雕塑艺术史不可或缺的珍贵实物资料。

15. 陶文俑头像　唐代
Pottery Figurine, Tang Dynasty

16. 陶侏儒俑　唐代
Pottery Midget, Tang Dynasty

17. 陶男俑(一) 唐代
Pottery Man(Ⅰ),Tang Dynasty

18. 陶男俑(二)　唐代
Pottery Man(Ⅱ),Tang Dynasty

19. 陶男俑(三)　唐代
Pottery Man(Ⅲ),Tang Dynasty

20. 陶男俑(四)　唐代
Pottery Man(Ⅳ),Tang Dynasty

21. 陶女俑　唐代
Pottery Woman, Tang Dynasty

22. 彩绘男侍陶俑(一)　唐代
Polychrome Male Servant Pottery Figurine(Ⅰ),
Tang Dynasty

23. 彩绘男侍陶俑(二) 唐代
Polychrome Male Servant Pottery Figurine(Ⅱ),
Tang Dynasty

24. 彩绘男侍陶俑(三)　唐代
Polychrome Male Servant Pottery Figurine(Ⅲ),
Tang Dynasty

25. 彩绘男侍陶俑(四)　唐代
Polychrome Male Servant Pottery Figurine(Ⅳ),
Tang Dynasty

26. 彩绘男侍陶俑(五)　唐代
Polychrome Male Servant Pottery Figurine(Ⅴ),
Tang Dynasty

27. 彩绘女侍陶俑(一)　唐代
Polychrome Maid Pottery Figurine(Ⅰ),
Tang Dynasty

28. 彩绘女侍陶俑(二)　唐代
Polychrome Maid Pottery Figurine(Ⅱ),
Tang Dynasty

29. 彩绘女侍陶俑(三)　唐代
Polychrome Maid Pottery Figurine(Ⅲ),
Tang Dynasty

30. 彩绘女侍陶俑(四)　唐代
Polychrome Maid Pottery Figurine(Ⅳ),
Tang Dynasty

31. 彩绘女侍陶俑(五) 唐代
Polychrome Maid Pottery Figurine(Ⅴ),
Tang Dynasty

32. 侍女陶俑　唐代
Pottery Handmaiden, Tang Dynasty

33. 陶鸡　唐代
Pottery Chicken, Tang Dynasty

34. 人物瓷俑(一)　宋代
Porcelain Figurine(Ⅰ),Song Dynasty

35. 人物瓷俑(二) 宋代
Porcelain Figurine(Ⅱ),Song Dynasty

36. 人物瓷俑(三)　宋代
Porcelain Figurine(Ⅲ),Song Dynasty

37. 人物瓷俑(四)　宋代
Porcelain Figurine(Ⅳ),Song Dynasty

铜器

铜器

Bronzeware

Bronzeware

1. 铜戣　周代
Bronze Lance,Zhou Dynasty

2. 蟠螭纹夔纹铜鼎　战国
Bronze Tripod with a Design of Curling Dragons,The Warring States

3. 错银铜车辖　战国
Silver-bronze Alloy Pin, The Warring States

4. 铜铃　战国
Bronze Bell, The Warring States

5. 铜戈(一)　战国
Bronze Dagger-Axe(Ⅰ),The Warring States

6. 铜戈(二)　战国
Bronze Dagger-Axe(Ⅱ),The Warring States

7. 铜戈(三)　战国
Bronze Dagger-Axe(Ⅲ), The Warring States

8. 铜鼎　西汉
Bronze Tripod, The Western Han Dynasty

9. 四蟠龙纹铜镜　西汉
Bronze Mirror with a Design of Four Dragons, The Western Han Dynasty

10. 铜舟　汉代
Bronze Container, Han Dynasty

11. 铜洗　汉代
Bronze Washing Pot, Han Dynasty

12. 铜壶　汉代
Bronze Kettle, Han Dynasty

13. 铜剑　汉代
Bronze Sword, Han Dynasty

14. 铜弩机　汉代
Bronze Cross-bow,Han Dynasty

15. 铜大吉铃　汉代
Big Bronze Bell, Han Dynasty

16. 规矩纹铜镜　汉代
Bronze Mirror with Regular Designs, Han Dynasty

17. 西王母人物铜镜　东汉
Bronze Mirror with Figure Patterns, The Eastern Han Dynasty

18. 对鸟纹铜镜　六朝
Bronze Mirror with a Design of Double Birds, The Six Dynasties

19. 五福双喜湖州造铜镜　宋代
Bronze Mirror of Double Happiness and Five Blessings Symbols Made in Hu Zhou,Song Dynasty

铜镜是古人照容饰面的生活用具，在我国已有四千多年的悠久历史。我国纪地、纪名号的铭镜最早出现在宋代。当时最著名的铸镜地区是以湖州为中心的浙江地区，故湖州镜在宋代是最为流行的镜类。铜镜上有产地及作坊字铭，下有把手应为手持之用，正中有一"囍"字，周边饰有纹样，有吉祥之寓意。

20. 荷花纹铜镜　宋代
Bronze Mirror with a Design of Lotus, Song Dynasty

21. 湖州石氏铜镜　宋代
Bronze Mirror Made by Shi Family from Hu Zhou, Song Dynasty

22. “无像”铜镜　宋代
Bronze Mirror, Song Dynasty

23.“广武县酒务记”铜印　宋代
Bronze Seal of “Alcohol Bureau of Guangwu County”,
Song Dynasty

24. “映湖”铜印　宋代
Bronze Seal of “Ying Hu”, Song Dynasty

25. 海兽葡萄纹镜　明代
Mirror with a Design of Sea Beast and Grapes, Ming Dynasty

26. 铜宣德炉(一)　清代
Bronze Censer from Emperor Xuande's Reign(Ⅰ),Qing Dynasty

27. 铜宣德炉(二)　清代
Bronze Censer from Emperor Xuande's Reign(Ⅱ),Qing Dynasty

28. 铜宣德炉(三)　清代
Bronze Censer from Emperor Xuande's Reign(Ⅲ),Qing Dynasty

29. 大刀(一)　清代
Broadsword(Ⅰ),Qing Dynasty

30. 大刀(二)　清代
Broadsword(Ⅱ),Qing Dynasty

玉器

玉器

Jadeware

Jadeware

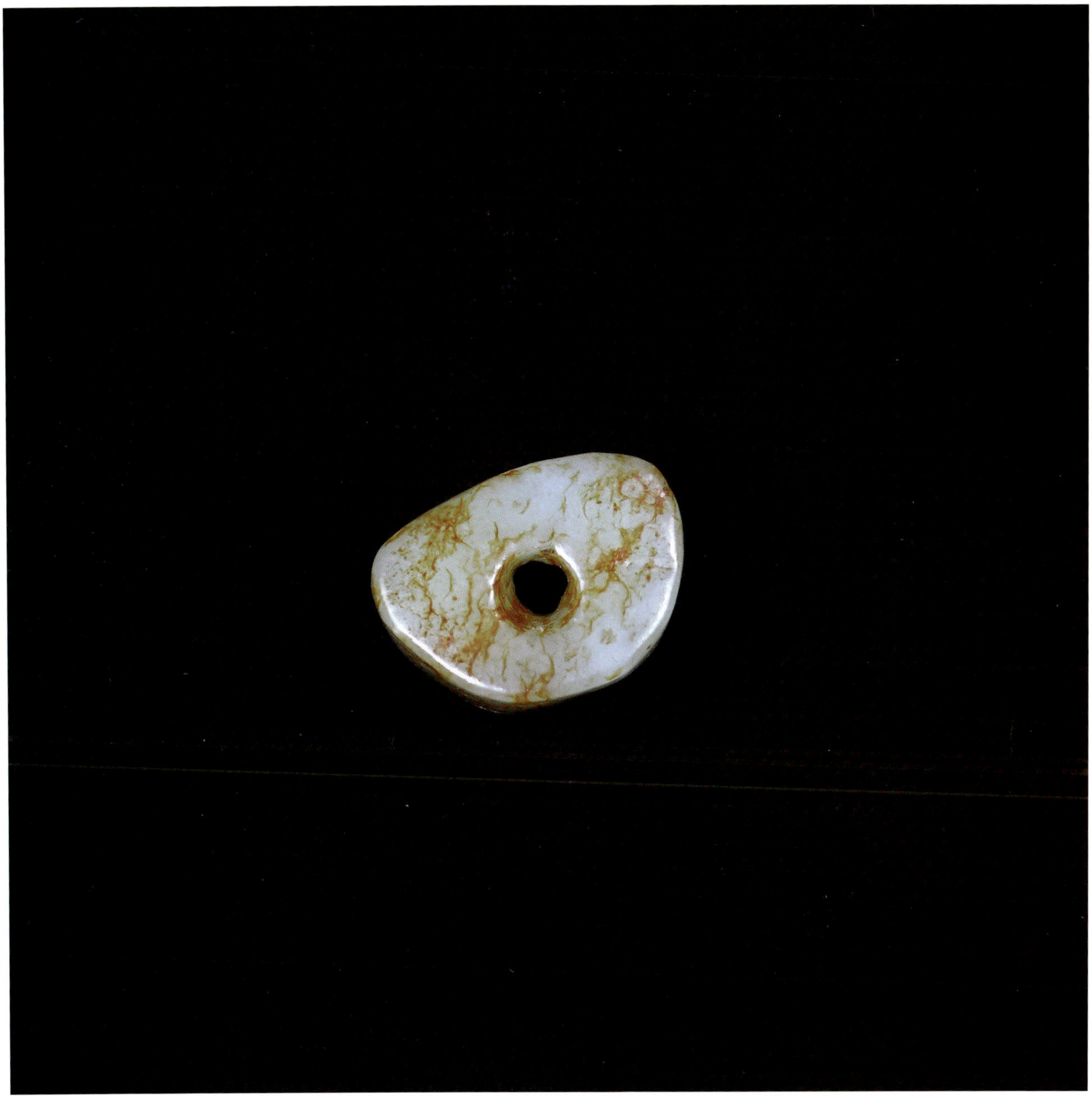

1. 玉佩饰　商代
Jade Pendant，Shang Dynasty

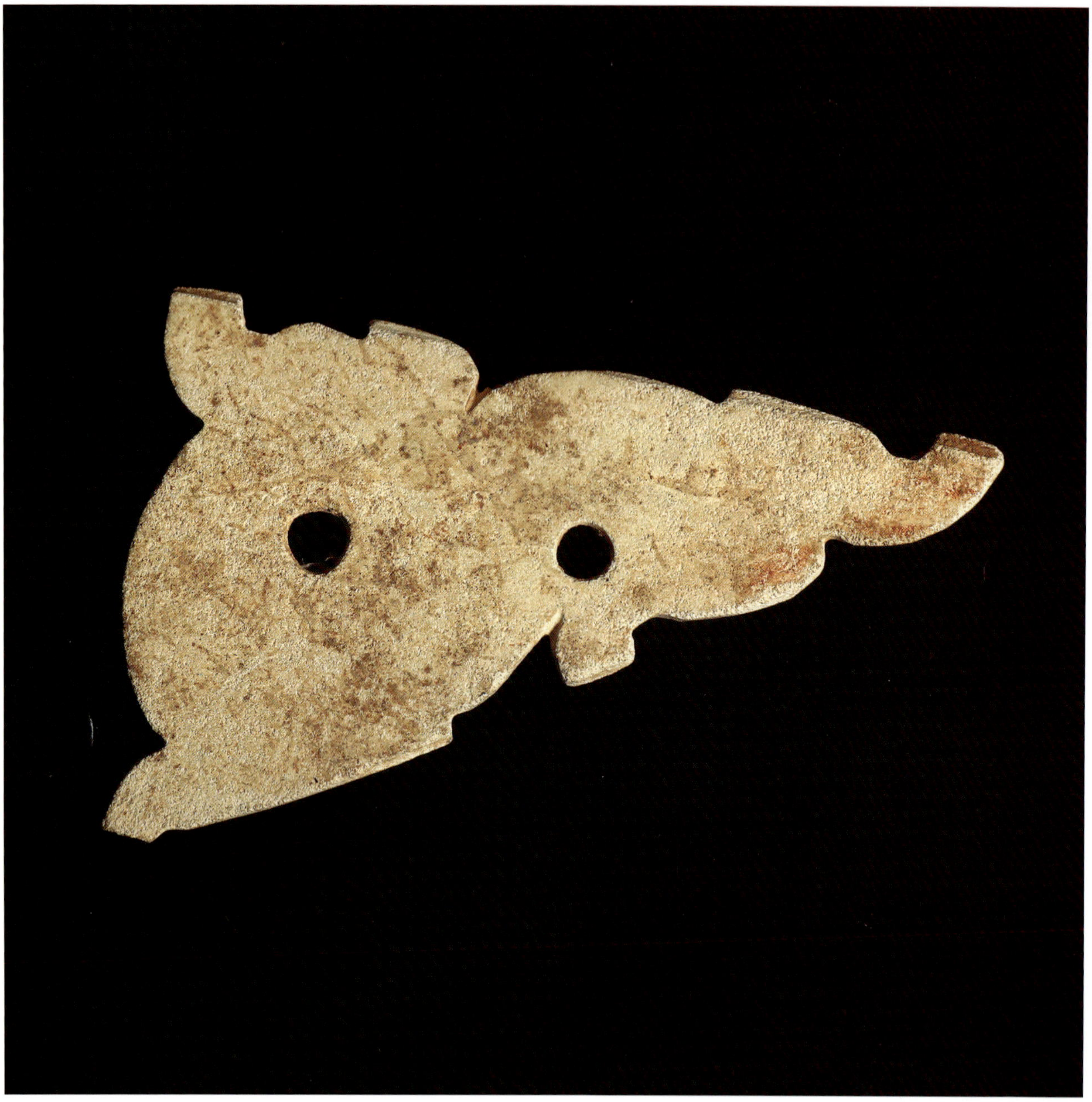

2. 玉瑱　商代
Jade Ornaments of Crown, Shang Dynasty

3. 玉谷纹璧　战国
Grain-patterned Jade Ornament, The Warring States

《尔雅》有云："肉倍好谓之璧"。肉即边，好即孔径，边是孔径的两倍便是璧，此璧完全符合形制。玉质通透，散布水银沁，璧上镌刻有成排的密集小乳丁，乳丁上雕成旋涡状如同谷芽，取其"谷可养生"之意。

4. 玉压脐　汉代
Jade Ornament, Han Dynasty

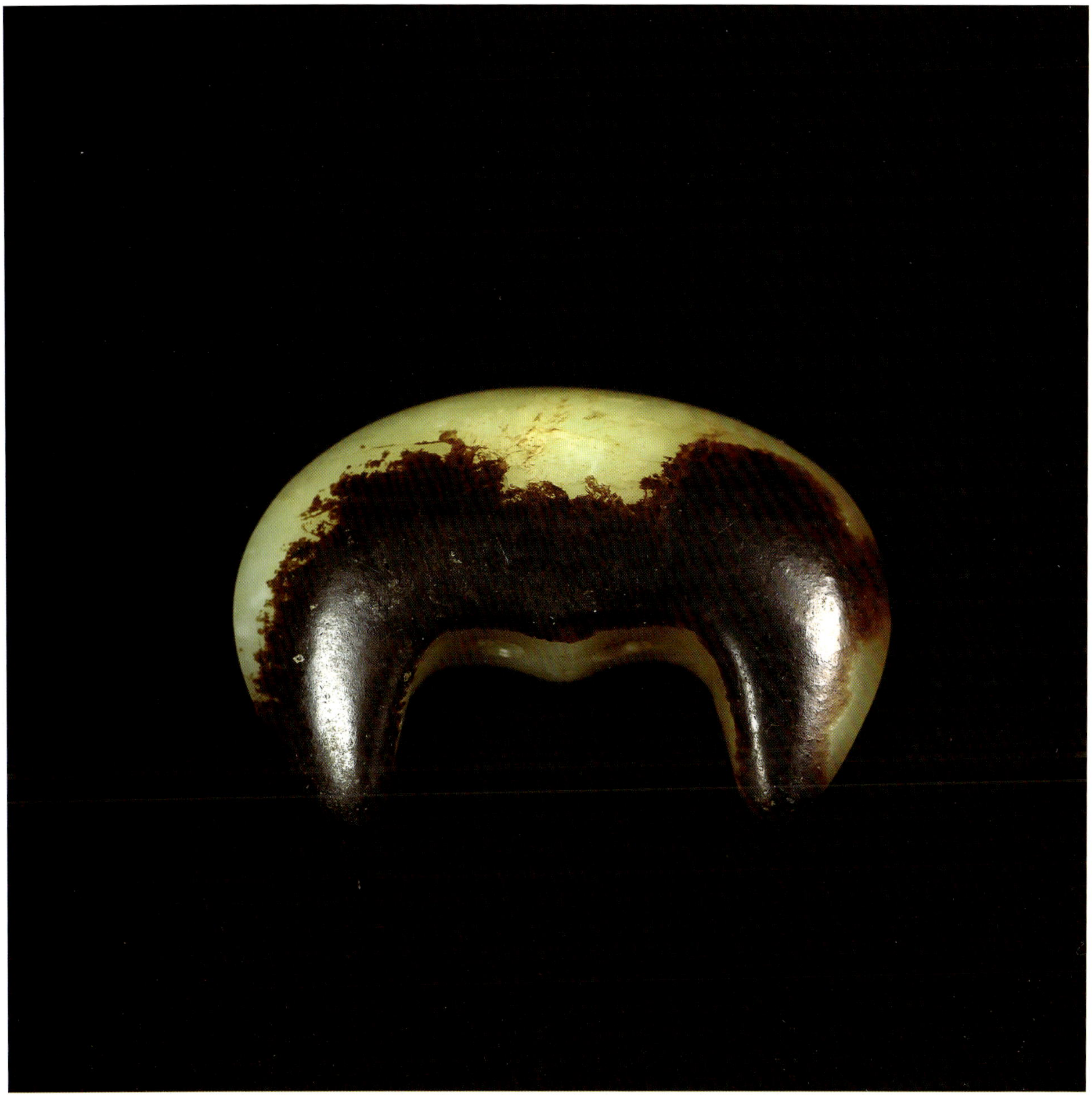

5. 玉饰　汉代
Jade Ornament, Han Dynasty

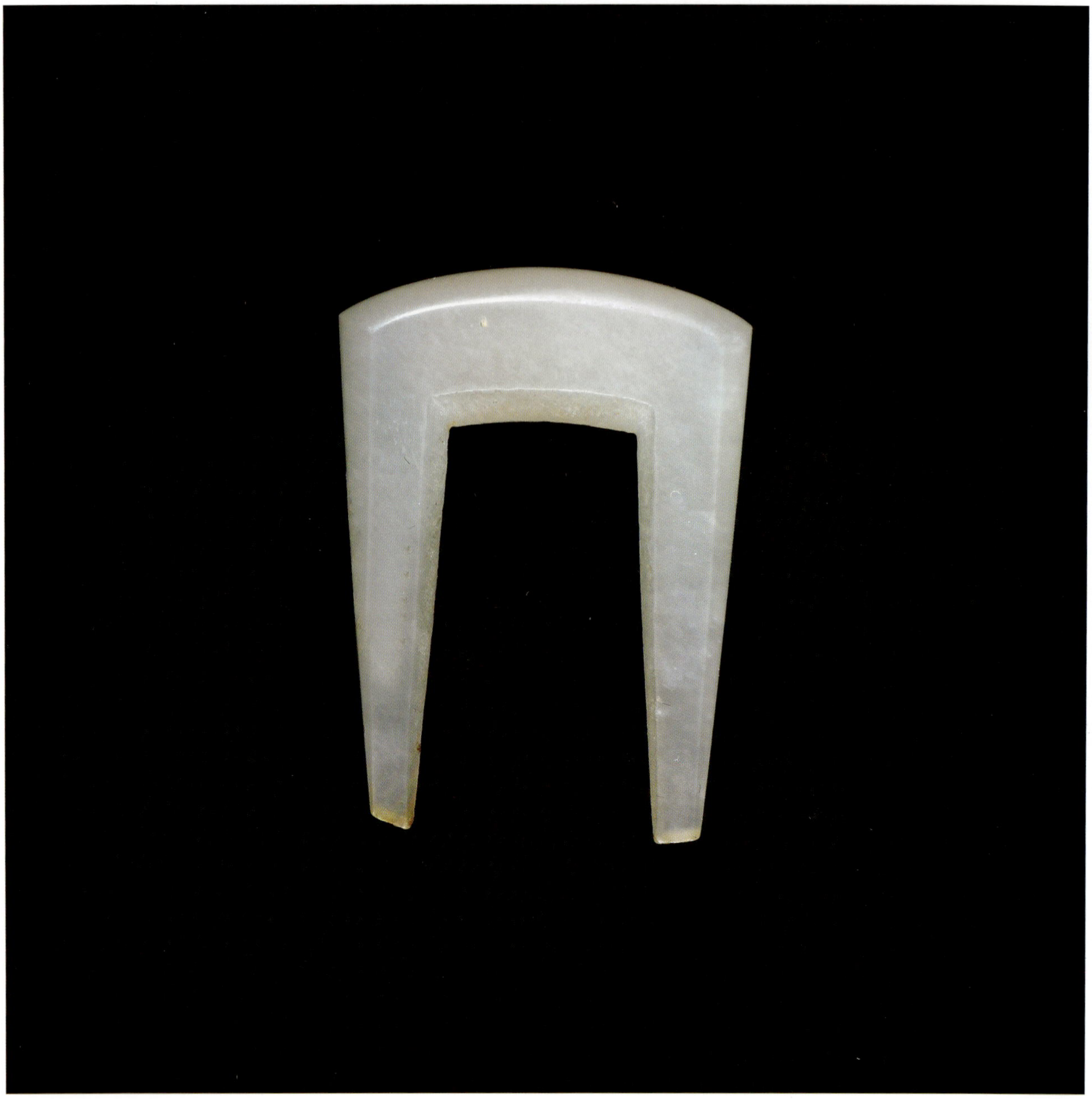

6. “∏”形玉饰　汉代
Jade Ornament, Han Dynasty

7. 玉马　南朝
Jade Horse, Southern Dynasty

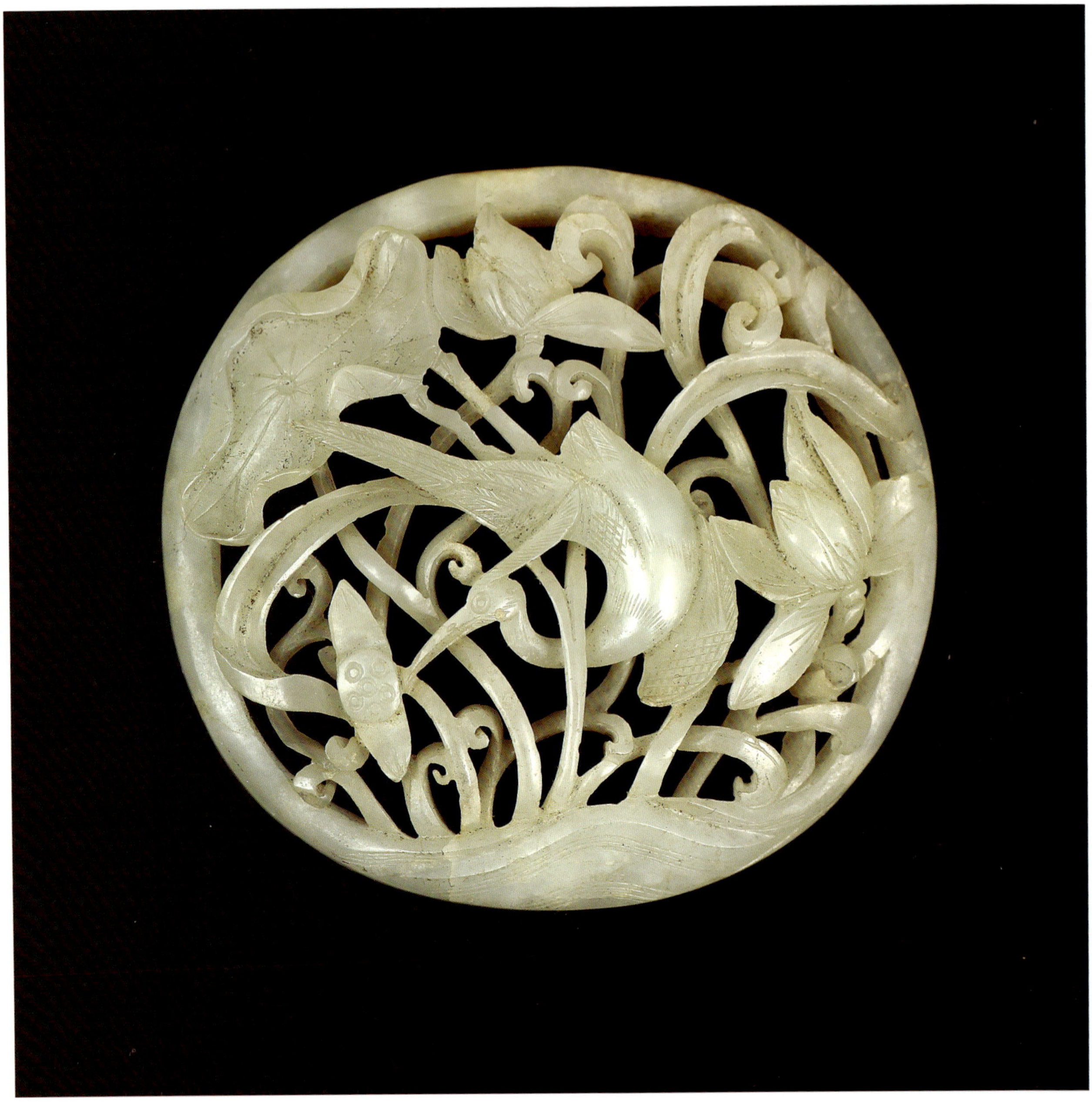

8. 玉雕鹭鸶荷花片　明代
Jade Egret and Lotus, Ming Dynasty

明代玉器渐趋脱离五代、两宋玉器形神兼备的艺术传统，形成了追求精雕细琢装饰美的艺术风格。明代的皇家用玉都由御用监监制，而民间观玉、赏玉之风盛行，在经济、文化发达的大城市中都开有玉肆，最著名的碾玉中心是苏州。

9. 玉龙纹透雕牌　明代
Jade Sculpture of Dragon, Ming Dynasty

10. 玉斋戒片　清代
Jade Plate, Qing Dynasty

11. 玉鲤鱼跳龙门纹璧　清代
Carp-through-Dragon-Gate Jade Ornament, Qing Dynasty

12. 玉环柄杯　清代
Jade Cup with Annular Handle, Qing Dynasty

13. 玉寿星　清代
Jade Figurine of God of Longevity, Qing Dynasty

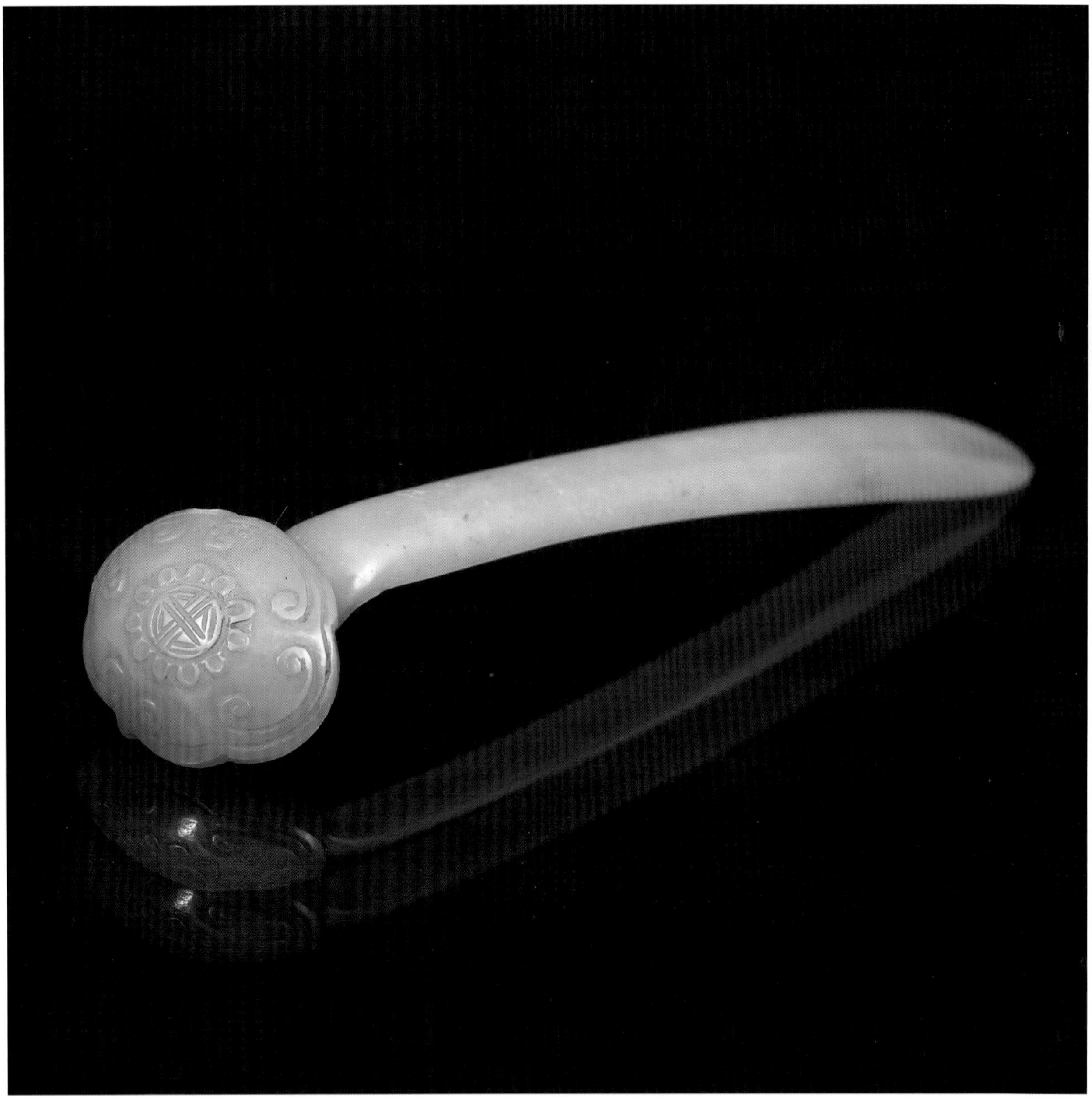

14. 玉如意　清代
Jade Symbol of Luck, Qing Dynasty

钱币

钱币

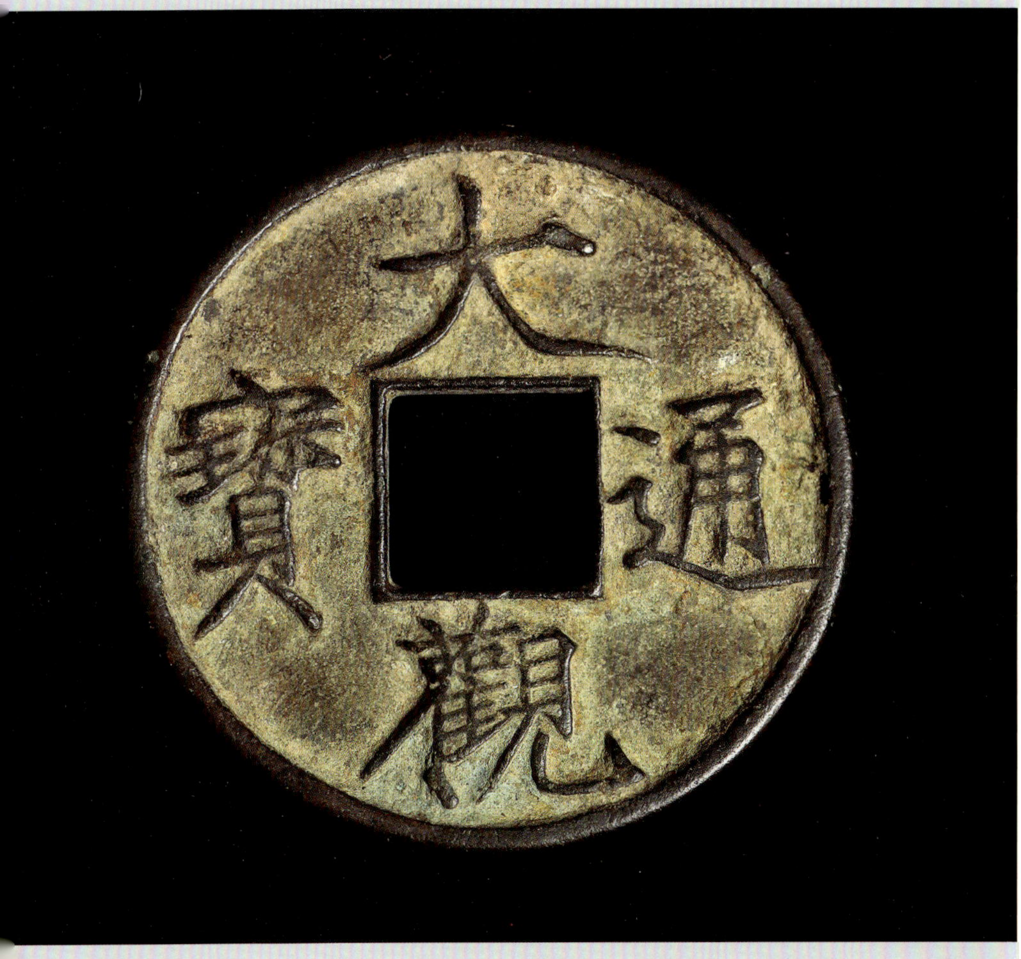

Coin

Coin

1. 安邑布币　战国
Cloth Currency of An Yi, The Warring States

2. 五字刀(即墨之法化)　战国
Bronze Knife-shaped Money, The Warring States

3.“垣”字钱币　战国
“Yuan” Character Coin, The Warring States

4. “大泉五十”钱范　新莽
Coin Mould of “Da Quan Fifty”,Wangmang’s New Dynasty

5. 大观通宝　宋代
Coin of Emperor Daguan's Reign, Song Dynasty

6. 洪武通宝　明代
Coin of Emperor Hongwu's Reign, Ming Dynasty

7. 太平天国铜钱　清代
Bronze Coin of The Taiping Heavenly Kingdom, Qing Dynasty

杂项

Sundries

1. 骨珠　商代
Bone Bead, Shang Dynasty

2. 骨簪　商代
Bone Hairpin, Shang Dynasty

3. 绳纹陶井圈　汉代
Ceramic Rope-worn Design Well-Crib,Han Dynasty

4. 铜佛像(一)　北朝
Bronze Statue of Buddha(Ⅰ), Northern Dynasty

5. 铜佛像(二) 北朝
Bronze Statue of Buddha(Ⅱ),Northern Dynasty

6. 铜佛像(三)　北朝
Bronze Statue of Buddha(Ⅲ),Northern Dynasty

7. 鎏金铜佛像　北朝
Gilded Bronze Statue of Buddha, Northern Dynasty

8. 隋开皇二年石佛造像　隋代
Buddha Stone Statue from the Second Year of Kai Huang Period, Sui Dynasty

9. 鎏金铜佛造像　北宋
Gilded Bronze Statue of Buddha, The Northern Song Dynasty

10. 骨蟠龙方牌　明代
Plate with a Design of Curling Dragon, Ming Dynasty

11. 陶龛　明代
Pottery Niche, Ming Dynasty

12. 筒瓦砚　清代乾隆年间
Inkstone, Qianlong's Reign of Qing Dynasty

13. 木雕观音像　清代
Wood Statue of Goddess of Mercy, Qing Dynasty

14. 竹雕花鸟压纸　清代
Bamboo Paperweight with a Design of Flowers and Birds, Qing Dynasty

15. 螺钿盘　清代
Plate Inlaid with Mother-of-pearl, Qing Dynasty

16. 木尺　清代
Wood Ruler, Qing Dynasty

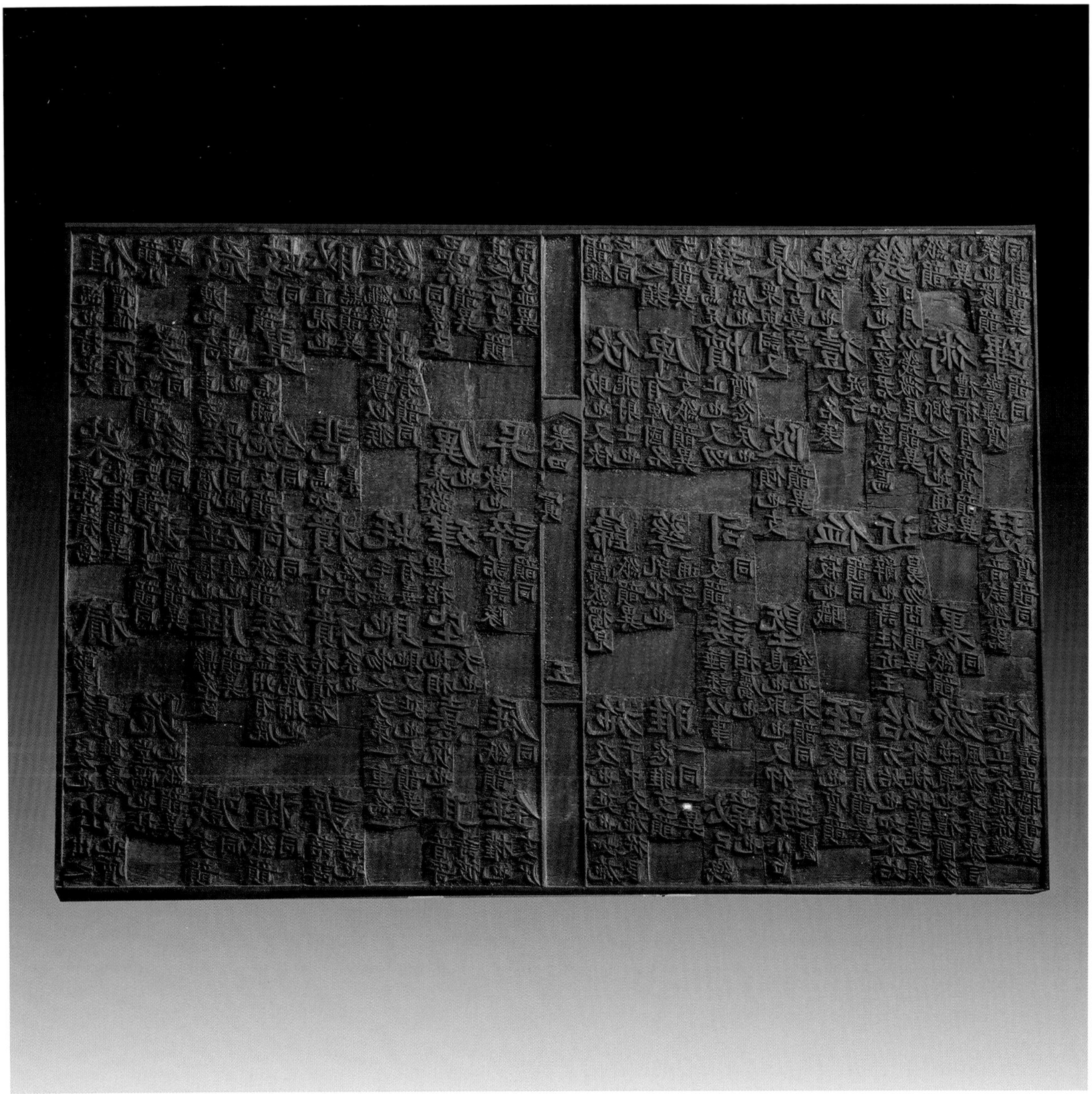

17. 字典木刻板(一)　清代
Wood Mould of Dictionary(Ⅰ),Qing Dynasty

18. 字典木刻板(二)　清代
Wood Mould of Dictionary(Ⅱ),Qing Dynasty

19. 吴大澂所用石砚　清代
Wu Dacheng's Inkstone, Qing Dynasty

参 考 文 献
References

1.《中国美术家人名词典》,上海人民出版社,1985年4月。

Name of Chinese Artist Dictionary,1985,Shanghai People's Publishing House.

2.《辞海》,夏征农,陈至立主编,上海辞书出版社,2010年4月第1版。

Cihai,Xia Zhengnong,Chen Zhili,2010,The Shanghai Lexicographical Publishing House.

3.《古今汉语字典》,商务印书馆辞书研究中心编,商务印书馆,2003年1月第1版。

Ancient and Modern Chinese Dictionary,The Center for Lexicographical Studies of the Commercial Press,2003,The Commercial Press.

4.《繁简字对照字典》,苏培成编,语文出版社,2007年7月第1版。

Complex Characters-Simplified Characters Dictionary,Su Peicheng,2007,Language and Literature Press.

5.《简化字繁体字对照字典》,江蓝生,陆尊梧编著,上海辞书出版社,2007年6月第1版。

Complex Characters-Simplified Characters Dictionary,Jiang Lansheng,Lu Zunwu,2007,The Shanghai Lexicographical Publishing House.

6.《隶书异体字字典》,张同标编著,河南美术出版社,2006年12月第2版。

Dictionary of Clerical Script Variants,Zhang Tongbiao,2006,Henan Fine Arts Publishing House.

7.《篆书异体字字典》,张同标编著,河南美术出版社,2007年4月第1版。

Dictionary of Seal Character Variants,Zhang Tongbiao,2007,Henan Fine Arts Publishing House.

8.《草书异体字字典》,张同标编著,河南美术出版社,2004年4月第1版。

Dictionary of Cursive Script Variants,Zhang Tongbiao,2004,Henan Fine Arts Publishing House.

9.《楷书异体字字典》,张同标编著,河南美术出版社,2006年12月第2版。

Dictionary of Regular Script Variants,Zhang Tongbiao,2006,Henan Fine Arts Publishing House.

10.《中华文化辞典》,冯天瑜主编,武汉大学出版社,2001年9月第1版。

Dictionary of Chinese Culture,Feng Tianyu,2001,Wuhan University Press.